OGHENETHOJA UMUTEME

UNDERSTAND *your* DESTINY

OGHENETHOJA UMUTEME

UNDERSTAND *your* DESTINY

MEMOIRS

Cirencester

Published by Memoirs

MEMOIRS
PUBLISHING

Memoirs Books
1A The Wool Market, Cirencester, Gloucestershire, GL7 2PR
info@memoirsbooks.co.uk | www.memoirspublishing.com

Understand your destiny (c)Oghenethoja Umuteme,
First published in England, 2015

ISBN 978-1-90987-482-4

Unless otherwise indicated, Bible quotations are taken from the King James Version. Scripture quotations marked with ESV, are taken from The Holy Bible, English Standard Version® (ESV®)_Copyright © 2001 by Crossway, a publishing ministry of Good News Publishers. All rights reserved.

All rights reserved. No part of this book shall be reproduced or transmitted in any form or by any means, electronic or mechanical, including photocopying, recording, or any information storage and retrieval system, without permission in writing from the copyright owner.

Address all enquiries to the publisher; Restoration Media House Limited
+234-8101700665, +2348076190064,
Email: rmhltd.info@gmail.com

Although the author and publisher have made every effort to ensure that the information in this book was correct when going to press, we do not assume and hereby disclaim any liability to any party for any loss, damage, or disruption caused by errors or omissions, whether such errors or omissions result from negligence, accident, or any other cause.
The views expressed in this book are purely the author's.

Printed in England

DEDICATION

To my students at the Christ Movement School of Ministry.
You have always wanted to know what it takes to fulfil and understand
one's destiny – now, here it is!

CONTENTS

	Introduction	
Chapter 1	A Destiny Is Born	Page 1
Chapter 2	The Facts You Need To Know	Page 20
Chapter 3	Saved To Save Others	Page 29
Chapter 4	Now Is The Hour!	Page 36
Chapter 5	Born To Experience Favour	Page 42
Chapter 6	Strive To Live Your Destiny In The Lord	Page 51
Chapter 7	The Place Of Education	Page 61
Chapter 8	Heaven's Gate Beckons - Hell's Gate Opens	Page 70
Chapter 9	Religion Is Sin Against Destiny	Page 81
Chapter 10	Keys To Living A Fulfilling Destiny	Page 93
Chapter 11	Ninety Per Cent Spiritual, Ten Per Cent Social	Page 99
Chapter 12	How You Have Fared	Page 103
Chapter 13	See Your Destiny Through The Eyes Of Others	Page 114
Chapter 14	Be Bold And Confront Your Fears	Page 120
Chapter 15	Getting Hold Of Time Before The Sun Sets	Page 145
	Covenant Confession	Page 161
	About The Author	Page 163

INTRODUCTION

～

An old man sat on the side of the bed, the thought of death nagging at his mind. All his age group were dead. He had been watching their burial video throughout the day.

He picked up his Bible, and opened it freely, and his eyes alighted on the passage in Genesis 40 when Jacob said his bones should be gathered and buried with those of his fathers. He closed the Bible quickly, then slowly again, freely, he opened the Bible, and his eyes noticed the dry bones in the valley in Ezekiel's vision.

Sweat drops, hot as boiling water, dropped from his face. Was he dying? He thought deeply. He had a lot to do, from forgiving and being forgiven to blessing his children. He also had to make some confessions. He packed everything he had laboured for; through and through he searched for the documents of all his possessions. Then his eyes caught the receipt for the radio set he had bought, the very first of his possessions, which was about 70 years old now. He reached out to get the radio, looking at how old it had become and old fashioned, yet still blaring. Then, quietly, he heard – 'is this all you spent your life on?'

If God were to ask us to list our achievements on Earth, would they be our cars, clothes, houses, etc? The Bible says the standard test would be fire – 1 Corinthians 3:12-13: ... *because it shall be revealed by fire; and the fire shall try every man's work of what sort it is.* We know that all material wealth can be destroyed by fire, implying that our destiny is more than earthly possessions.

In 1631 Robert Barker and Martin Lucas, two of London's most respected book printers, produced a reproduction of the King James version of the Bible and omitted the word "not" in the 7th commandment in Exodus 20:14, so instead of reading *"Thou shall not commit adultery"*, it read *"Thou shall commit adultery"*. This version of the Holy Bible has come to be known as the Wicked Bible, also called the Adulterous Bible or Sinners' Bible. Though their action was not intentional, this single typographical error caused significant distress in the religious community, since it could conceivably be interpreted as holy permission to commit a sinful act.

King Charles 1 of England and George Abbot, the Archbishop of Canterbury in 1631, summoned the two men, fined them £300 and withdrew their printing licences. The copies of this Bible were burnt, leaving only 11 copies. One copy is in the collection of rare books in the New York Public Library and is very rarely made accessible; another can be seen in the Bible Museum in Branson, Missouri. The British Library in London had a copy on display in a free exhibition until September 2009.

This typographical error was considered an unforgivable sin against the Holy word of God. Only God knows how many people were led astray by this omission, and their destinies put on hold. If this omission attracted the attention and punishment above, what shall we do to those who on daily basis interprets the Bible to suite their selfish desires? Today we have pastors and preachers who have taught their congregations with their man-made doctrines leading to moral decadence in all spheres of our society.

* * *

A UK *Independent* newspaper headline on Tuesday, 16 February 1993 read 'Nurse killed children in her care on

Ward 4'. Over 59 days, four children were murdered and nine were victims of hospital attacks, the court was told - *http://www.independent.co.uk*

I got this profile of the nurse from the Murderpedia website: http://murderpedia.org/female.A/a/allitt-beverley.htm:

- Name: Beverley Gail ALLITT (A.K.A.: "Angel of Death")
- Classification: Serial killer
- Characteristics: Nurse suffering from the mental illness Munchausen's Syndrome by Proxy
- Number of victims: 4
- Date of murders: February-April 1991
- Date of arrest: November 1991
- Date of birth: October 4, 1968
- Victim's profiles: Liam Taylor, 7-months-old, Timothy Hardwick, 11 years old, Becky Phillips, 2 months old, Claire Peck, 15 months old.
- Method of murder: Poisoning (insulin - lignocaine)
- Location: Lincolnshire, England, United Kingdom
- Status: Sentenced to 13 concurrent terms of life imprisonment on May 28, 1993.

The website went on to say about her – 'Beverly Allitt, better known as the "Angel of Death", is one of Britain's most notorious female serial killers. Her murderous spree was all the more shocking because she would befriend the parents of her victims who entrusted their children into her care.

As a child, Beverly would use factitious injuries in order to gain attention. She took to wearing bandages and casts over "wounds" but would not allow them to be examined. As a teenager, an overweight Beverly began spending an excessive amount of time in hospitals with numerous physical complaints. At one point she persuaded a surgeon to remove a perfectly healthy appendix. When they realized what she was doing she would doctor-shop, moving on from one physician to the next.

She attended Grantham College in Lincolnshire and trained as a nurse. Her bizarre behaviour continued throughout her training. While working at a nursing home she was suspected of smearing faeces on the walls. Her attendance during her training was poor due to her many illnesses and as a result she failed her nursing examinations. Still she was able to obtain a position at Grantham and Kesteven Hospital in Lincolnshire in 1991 as a State Enrolled Nurse. Beverly was assigned to Children's Ward 4.'

Surprising, how an unqualified nurse got employed, and the result is mass killing of innocent children. These destinies have been terminated.

***

A car left the road and went on into the river. People ran to rescue the passengers, but they were all dead at the point of rescue. Destinies terminated again!

***

Beside a rail track lays a dead rat. The rail maintenance team swept it into the nearby bush. As they did that, they saw a snake coiled up. Wondering what the snake was busy with, one of the workers threw a stick at it; the snake didn't respond. He threw another stick at it, and the snake uncoiled itself and slid into the bush. Afraid, the worker cautioned the other workers to avoid being too close to the bush to prevent be beaten by the snake. One could see 'caution' boldly written on their faces.

As they hurriedly carried out their duty, one of the workers called out that there was another rat lying dead by the rail track. It was obvious the snake was the culprit. In the distance they could sense an object crossing the rail track, and they wondered if a train was passing. Just then they heard the blaring of the train horn and they hurried away from the rail track. The train came by and someone dropped a leaflet down through the window, and the caption read – 'Do you bother about them too?' The workers passed it round and they all read it. With one voice, they exclaimed 'Yes we do!' They rushed into the nearby bush with sticks in their hand, and hunted down the snake.

***

I had just completed my twelfth book, *The Mystery of the Kingdom of God on Earth*, and sent it to my editor. I relaxed on a sofa in my sitting room, happy that the book was completed and ready to get some nights of sleep. My students in the 'Certificate in Ministry' class had come and were waiting for me to teach them. Then I heard – 'Understand your destiny.' The voice repeated the same words again after some time. I looked at the time, it was 5pm; I got myself up and went to teach my students. The more I was there teaching, the more this subject was occupying my mind. Then I heard:

Your destiny is in your hands.

A chase in the right direction will take you to your destination.

I knew it was time for another training session with my Teacher – The Holy Spirit.

Pst. Oghenethoja Umuteme
President/Founder
Royal Diamonds Int'l Church
(Christ Movement)
Port Harcourt, Nigeria.

CHAPTER ONE

A DESTINY IS BORN

'I have suffered!' My mum said as she recounted how she had suffered before and after she married my dad. 'I suffered as a child,' she continued. 'My mum woke up one morning and saw my leg on fire. I was sleeping close to her, the fire had been put up to keep us warm, this was not the first day though, but somehow my leg got into the fire. I cried in anguish while my mother slept, and when she finally woke up, she cried for help. My leg was already burnt' She pointed to her legs. 'Here is the mark of the burn I received' she lamented. She shook her head and sighed. 'Well such is life, I am still alive today to see my children grow.'

While I ponder over the story of the pain she went through, she started off, 'the woman that threw my leg into fire confessed that she was a witch and wanted to

CHAPTER ONE

end my life. After her confession, she died mysteriously and all her children have become wayward also. I have seen that evil doesn't pay. All those who perpetrated evil while I was growing up as a child are now dead.

'As if that was not enough' she continued, 'when I married your father I became barren for eight years – my bags were continuously thrown out of your father's house by his relatives but my husband, your father, has always been by my side. Then one afternoon, while in the farm, the rains started falling and a man ran into our hut. He looked at me and smiled, and then he asked, "Where are your children?" I shook my head and started crying. He told me he could see seven children around me but what was holding them was the mystery that must be resolved.

'Later the rain stopped and he went into the forest. I wept bitterly while your father consoled me. Then on another occasion, the strange man showed up again, this time telling us that he had discussed with the perpetrator of the wicked act of making me barren. The man was a neighbour nearby.

'True to his word, I became pregnant. During the period I was pregnant with you, I experienced serious trials. Sometimes people would engage me in a quarrel so that a fight could ensue for them to have an excuse to hit me so that my womb would bleed and finally become a miscarriage. Somehow, your God has always delivered you.'

My father had been away. The moon was beaming down with a generous smile and her light was gaining forceful control over the darkness of the night. People could see clearly now. Then my father came in. He saw me sitting attentively listening to my mum. After understanding the purpose of the discussion she was having with me, he sat down by her and started.

'My son,' he looked up and sighed, 'life is so funny, that even today I am a father to you and your siblings. Shortly after your mother became pregnant and you were bouncing in her womb, we went through hell in the hands of some people. The funny part was that all of them knew you were going to be a boy, I don't know how. Well, I was a hunter and on this fateful night I set out to hunt for game. Just as I went into the forest, I saw an antelope gazing at me, which was unusual. There was cold all over my body when I saw it. I was dead afraid. I tried to avoid the antelope, but it kept following me wherever I went in the forest and would always be gazing at me. I tried to pull the trigger on the gun, but the cold

CHAPTER ONE

that enveloped me was too much for me to bear. I pulled myself together and decided to return home while the antelope continuously showed up until I left the forest and went back home. The cold was all over me till the morning.

'When later I came out, I met an old man who told me all I had gone through in the forest and concluded that I would have killed my son if I had shot that antelope. The antelope was manipulated to represent the child in the womb so that I would have been held accountable for killing my own son had I shot at the antelope. After that I swore not to go hunting again.'

Just then my mum added, 'the man that tied my womb confessed some years back how he tied my womb, and since then he has died mysteriously. He was actually the tailor that made my wedding clothes, the wrapper and the blouse, and I have kept them here waiting for this night.' She went inside and brought out the white lace wrapper and blouse. 'Here they are.' She gave them to me. 'The witch actually took a piece from this cloth to tie my womb. Human beings are wicked. But today he is dead.'

This story launched me into the deep spiritual insight I have into issues today. Right from that night I have

CHAPTER ONE

never been the same. This story is actually the reason behind my quest for the ultimate power, which I later found in the Bible. This is because shortly after they recounted their story, the devil roared again and wanted to turn my life into that of a wayward son. I thank God my mum and dad told me this story, as otherwise I would have dined with Satan.

I have recounted this story here because many don't believe in satanic manipulations. This book is for those seeking restoration and as you soak yourself in this elaborate teaching, you shall experience restoration in full.

The words of Jesus in Matthew 26:39 explain something about why we are here on Earth: *O my Father, if it be possible, let this cup pass from me: nevertheless not as I will, but as thou wilt.* The word 'nevertheless' shows that it is pointless trying to have our own way. God controls everything, and that explains His sovereignty over the universe.

Many times we are bugged with the fact of trying to seek out our purpose on Earth. We are often seen praying and asking God for direction. To explain this fact, the Lord said in Isaiah 42:9,16: *Behold, the former things are come to pass, and new things do I declare: before they*

CHAPTER ONE

spring forth I tell you of them. And I will bring the blind by a way that they knew not; I will lead them in paths that they have not known: I will make darkness light before them, and crooked things straight. These things will I do unto them, and not forsake them. What are the new things that He wants to declare unto us? What are the former things that have been fulfilled? How did we become blind when we have our eyes wide open? Which way is He leading us through? Where are we heading to in this new way? What crooked things will be made straight as we walk with the Lord? Did He forsake us before? If He did forsake us, what did we do wrong?

These and many questions would be running through our minds right now. The fact remains that we have a destined path to walk on, which is the path of life that will make us do the will of God here on Earth. The Bible is clear about this as posited by the following two verses, Exodus 23:20, Isaiah 30:21: *Behold, I send an Angel before thee, to keep thee in the way, and to bring thee into the place which I have prepared. And thine ears shall hear a word behind thee, saying, This is the way, walk ye in it, when ye turn to the right hand, and when ye turn to the left.* It is this way that the Lord is leading us that explains the fact that we are born with a divine destiny, which

CHAPTER ONE

leads to our destination. There is a place prepared for each and every one of us, and if we are not on the right track, the Lord is going to call out some day as He did to Abraham – Genesis 12:1: *Now the Lord had said unto Abram, Get thee out of thy country, and from thy kindred, and from thy father's house, unto a land that I will shew thee.* Severally we would see the Lord calling out to people to follow Him, and so did He raise His disciples. Our destiny points to the purpose and plan of God for this world. Buttressing this fact, Jesus had this to say,– John 9:4: *I must work the works of him that sent me, while it is day: the night cometh, when no man can work.* In complaining of this fact that many have abandoned their destiny, the word of the Lord says, Isaiah 42:22: ... *none saith, Restore.* The urgency of the work of God is so important that Christ would say, Matthew 8:22: *Follow me; and let the dead bury their dead.*

A distress call is received from the Earth. The call is analysed and Angels sent to explore and confirm what sort of call it was and to verify the authenticity of the call. The Angels come back with reports of events on the face of the Earth – murder, idolatry, fornication, adultery, corruption and all manner of carnal desires. The reports are delivered in specific terms – location, the age of those

CHAPTER ONE

involved, etc, thus explaining the fact that they have abandoned their duty call on Earth. A deliverer would be sent to that zone with the message of repentance on his lips. The process begins with the host of heaven looking for a couple through whom this deliverer will be sent into the Earth. Once such is located, the Lord begins the forming process – Jeremiah 1:5: *Before I formed thee in the belly I knew thee; and before thou camest forth out of the womb I sanctified thee, and I ordained thee a prophet unto the nations.* Nine months later, the child will be given birth to, and his parents would christen him with a name they had received from the Lord. As time goes on, the child grows in the specific environment where the distress call was sent from, learning about their ways of lives, and seldom seen confronting the evil practices of these people. Occasionally he would be seen with group of people where he would try to win their opinion as to what he feels is the solution to the problem in their society. He would be hated, and attacked by those who feel his lifestyle was odd and awkward to the status quo.

This deliverer would often be at loggerheads with his parents too, and in the face of his rejection, he will seek solace in the Lord and then the Lord will tell him who he is and what he is to do. Often they would complain – Jeremiah 1:6: *Ah, Lord God! behold, I cannot speak: for I am a child.* In the face of this, the Lord will reaffirm His backing – Jeremiah 1:7-8: *Say not, I am a child: for thou shalt go to all that I shall send thee, and whatsoever I command thee thou shalt speak. Be not afraid of their faces: for I am with thee to deliver thee, saith the Lord.*

Where is the Lord sending him to? First, it is to those in authority, who have misled His children out of their ordained destiny to serve the Lord and do His will. So he meets with more confrontations, more frowning faces, more hatred, more betrayers, etc. The reason is simply because his actions would take food from the tables of the authorities in power, and set the children of God free, so that they can fulfil their destiny.

We would now see a few deliverers in the Bible:

Noah – Genesis 5:29: *And he called his name Noah, saying, 'this same shall comfort us concerning our work and toil of our hands, because of the ground which the Lord hath cursed.'* From this verse we see that the suffering upon the face of the Earth was so much as a result of the curse God laid on mankind in Genesis 3:17-19: *...cursed is the ground for thy sake; in sorrow shalt* *thou eat of it all the days of thy life; Thorns also and thistles shall it bring forth to thee; and thou shalt eat the herb of the field; In the sweat of thy face shalt thou eat bread...* It wouldn't be out of proportion if we say that mankind was facing extinction as a result of hard labour with little food to eat, as the land wasn't yielding its full strength. Sin multiplied upon the face of the Earth to the extent that Angels also left their duty (Genesis 6). There would be several distress calls then, from the Earth, and Noah was destined to carry out a mission of rescue, unto the glory of God.

David: He was the youngest in the family, yet he was sent into the wild to look after his father's flocks, and would time after time encounter wild animals that would have taken his life. This has often baffled me, why Jesse, David's father, would send a young defenceless lad into the field alone. His lonely nature may have been the reason why he developed interest in music at such an age that would earn him an employment in the house of the king Saul. We would also notice that most rejected and isolated people have become very creative and successful in music and other forms of creative arts. God chose him and anointed him. The anointing took him into

CHAPTER ONE

the house of Saul, king of Israel, at least, to understand the act of kingship. The anointing also took him to the war front where he defeated Goliath to the glory of God. His success brought him envy and his life was in danger again – first in the field, now in the safest home, the kings' palace, not out of selfish ambition, but for the defence of the people and the name of God. He took to the mountains and hills and wilderness to avoid death, and suffered a great deal despite the anointing upon him. The anointing brought him back into the palace again, now as a king. He fell into the temptation of adultery – the pleasure in the world, but was strengthened by God again, and he would rule Israel, pleasing the Lord and successfully handed over to a successor – his son, which was the first time in the land that a king would hand over to a successor while still alive.

The anointing makes the difference. Prayers are mere words until they are transformed into spiritual packets of thoughts. Revelations 8:3 says it all, as the Angels only offered the prayers of the saints to God. Can you see why God answers men of God quicker than those who are not filled with the anointing? How long will you pray without answers, or run from one prophet or church to

CHAPTER ONE

the other without fulfilment? The secret is in the anointing. In Psalm 89:20-33, David succeeded because the anointing was upon him.

My life is a living testimony of the Lord's anointing, and it is available for everyone. Once the anointing comes into your life, your complaints are changed into praise. Satan will discourage you from seeking God to the extent that you can receive the Holy Spirit, because he knows that the day you receive the Holy Spirit, from then onward, your stories will change. Be zealous for God, and He will come to you.

Have you ever imagined why Men of God are so respected, and they become so rich? It is the anointing. Have you ever wondered why Jesus was buried by a rich man in a fresh tomb that no one had been buried in before (Matthew 27:57-60, Mark 15:43-46 and Luke 23:5-53)? It is the respect for anointing! I came from a family of want, but God's anointing upon me has made the difference. Everything in my life is centred on the anointing. Desire the HOLY SPIRIT today and be anointed for EXPLOITS. It is the secret of the unseen power of God.

How many of us would agree that to fulfil our destinies we may have to undergo some form of life-saving

CHAPTER ONE

suffering experience? This is the beauty of a rescue mission. We put our lives in danger to save others who are already in danger. This is the beauty of destiny at work. On the 26th of September 2014, 5am, the Lord spoke to me: *'let them follow me and I will change them, the way you followed me and I changed your life.'* We cannot follow Jesus until we are ready to bear our own cross. Humility and loyalty set you on the pedestal of life - they give you the value that money cannot buy.

While I prayed for workers, some of those who came, though were ready to work, were not ready to follow process; they only wanted what God can give to them. Life becomes a mistake when we are unable to extract wisdom from the odd experiences we have gone through in life. Someone needs your success story to mend his/her ways and then become another success story. Don't live a life of sympathy. When you turn your disappointments into divine appointments you will become a teacher of experience, and you will become everyone's mentor of destiny. If you are raising others to work with you, ensure you do not cast fear into their heart. Always make them know they can do it. We were told that the moment Jesus stated to the Disciples what

He would endure at death, they became sorrowful and He could tell them no more secrets (John 16:6). With sorrow comes fear. But later Jesus promised them the Holy Spirit, and they became warm again.

It is worth noting that we all are sent into this world as deliverers, and because many of us haven't come to this reality and fact of life, we have not being able to fulfil our destiny. In the verse of Isaiah 42:16 we read earlier, we are told that two main factors are responsible for our inability to fulfil our destinies – **'spiritual blindness,'** and walking on **'crooked paths.'** We may now quickly see what this means. To be blind spiritually means that we are unable to connect with the light of God, which would mean that whatever we do, we will be groping, and thus living a stagnant, obscured life. Those who walk in darkness walk in fear because their boldness is taken away by unseen images manifesting in their hearts. They often trip while walking, and seldom get frustrated with life. The Lord says He turns our darkness into day – Isaiah 42:16. On the second part, crooked paths are time-consuming paths; they are taken through parabolic paths. Those who walk in crooked paths are those the Lord speak parables to, and as long as they are unable to decode the meaning of the parable, they are bound to remain deprived of heavenly secrets. This causes physical stagnation and deprivation.

So, the next time you hear that a child is born within your neighbourhood, you may just be seeing the deliverer you have so prayed for in your midst. We often look at the face of the child to know who it resembles, daddy's family or mummy's family, rather than thanking God the way Hannah did when Jesus was presented at the temple – Luke 2:38: *And she coming in that instant gave thanks likewise unto the Lord, and spake of him to all them that looked for redemption in Jerusalem.*

This explains the fact that we all are here on a mission – born with a mission, to salvage the Earth from eternal destruction. Though many of us have joined the devil to compound issues upon the face of the Earth for God, many have decided not to join any rescue team commissioned by the Lord, and have tried to live in isolation – sitting on the fence. While still others joined one of the teams and became carried away by worldly pleasures and are no longer fit for the rescue mission, some others still have been called back to the heavenly base after impressing the Lord.

CHAPTER ONE

Our destiny is our course on Earth. The day we were born, a destiny was born. We have all come into this world as answers to prayers sent into the realm of God by humans. The woman by the well said of the expected Messiah (John 4:25): *The woman saith unto him, I know that Messiahs cometh, which is called Christ: when he is come, he will tell us all things.* And Jesus indeed revealed all things concerning the purpose of creation. When Pilate asked Jesus if He was a king, this is what Jesus replied – John 18:37: *Thou sayest that I am a king. To this end was I born, and for this cause came I into the world, that I should bear witness unto the truth.* Jesus's destiny was to bear witness unto the truth. The world is suffering because of deceit and the devil has given men lying and deceitful tongues. Deceit is a soul-crushing venom targeted at your plans in life. Our destiny is to fulfil the wish of God for the Earth – Mark 8:33: *But when he had turned about and looked on his disciples, he rebuked Peter, saying, Get thee behind me, Satan: for thou savourest not the things that be of God, but the things that be of men.* And to ensure we carry out this onerous task of the Lord as apportioned to every one of us we are supposed to put on a form that fully aligns with the

CHAPTER ONE

purpose of heaven by receiving the Holy Spirit, and becoming born of the Spirit – John 3:8. With this we, being empowered by the Lord, will be able to destroy the works of the devil – 1 John 3:8: *For this purpose the Son of God was manifested, that he might destroy the works of the devil.* So you would see that the day you were born marked the beginning of Satan falling from whichever seat he is occupying in the vicinity of where you were born. Daniel was the only one who could read the handwriting on the wall: *mene, mene, tekel, upharsin* – Daniel 5:25. There is a spiritual handwriting on the wall waiting to be interpreted by you so that this world can be saved from the pit of hell. Angels can no longer walk the face of this earth as in the old because of high level of sin – murders of innocent souls and high levels of sexual immorality.

This is one clear reason why most successful people today in the world were born and raised by poor parents, and these people must fulfil this call of liberation from poverty with total submission to God, else they cannot return to God who sent them.

A husband may have been sent to deliver an entire family from pain, poverty, deprivation, etc., in the wife's family, but we would often see the man's family fighting this course. The wife may have been sent into a man's life to bring wealth into the family, in which case you will see the woman coming from a house of great wealth – and her parents would fight this course. How often have we fought against the wish of God?

To be able to fulfil this task before us, encapsulated in our destiny, we all must understand our purpose here on Earth, and continuously return to God, pointing everyone to Him so that we may live a life filled with His glory all the days of our lives.

If we would look deeply between the lines in the following Psalms we would identify what purpose we have come to fulfil here on Earth:

- God made us all – Psalm 139
- God teaches us and establishes us therewith – Psalm 119
- The Lord is our provider, and protection – Psalm 23
- We must pray and worship in His Altar – Psalm 28,42,60:4-5.
- We must be found serving in his court – Psalm 65:4
- We must act and live by the anointing character He has given to us – Psalm 89:20-23

CHAPTER ONE

Then, we please Him and fulfil our destiny on Earth – John 19:30, 2 Timothy 4:7.

Those who are not on the path of their destiny are filled with complaints and would be seen not to have satisfaction in whatever they are doing. This is why Christ came to give us the life we lost while we were in sin, so that we can abhor sin and live abundantly in Him (John 10:10), thus fulfilling out destiny. And for parents, I would encourage you to continually ask God the reason why He gave you the child that is with you now. And for many, who are yet to discover the path to their destiny, follow me as we explore further.

I would want you to use this prayer line – Lord, where have I missed it? Am I training my children in the right direction? Lord, please, lead me to the path of my destiny.

CHAPTER TWO

THE FACTS YOU NEED TO KNOW

Before we continue, now that we are aware that we are born to fulfil a destiny, we should discuss some facts we must know about destiny:

- We are the ones to map out the path to our destiny, and because it cannot be achieved by mere human wisdom, we would need the hand of the Almighty God, who created us, to help us in this destiny mapping-out strategy. Navigate your way back to your destiny today.

- Our destiny is covered in the terms of the covenant we enter with God. This is why we make vows before the Altar also, so that we would be empowered from above to enable us actualize our

CHAPTER TWO

destiny. In Genesis 6:18, God was specific about who the covenant will cover - *But with thee will I establish my covenant; and thou shalt come into the ark, thou, and thy sons, and thy wife, and thy sons 'wives with thee.* The covenant only got a boost from the Lord, with more promises after Noah had sacrificed unto to Lord – Genesis 9:9: *And I, behold, I establish my covenant with you, and with your seed after you.* Notice that in the first instance, God said *I will establish,* but after Noah sacrificed, God said *I establish.* In verse 11, God intensified the promise, and became more specific on who would be the covenant bearer -*And I will establish my covenant with you.* And for this sake, this reason, a mark was set in heaven – the rainbow, as a remembrance. This is the fact that Psalm 50:5 explains - *Gather my saints together unto me; those that have made a covenant with me by sacrifice.* If you want to fulfil your destiny, you must be covered by a covenant, and then you must become one who sacrifices for the work of God. We need to keep on reminding God of His covenant to deliver and help us as we fulfil our destiny. If we don't tell a teacher we are having problems, he will assume we understand all that he is teaching.

CHAPTER TWO

- The enemy can take ownership of our destiny, and will often use it to enrich themselves. This is the case with many artists all over the world – the aristocrats in society comes as wolves in sheep's clothing, pretending to help, yet only coming to exploit their God's given talents and destiny. If we look into all those who have made feats all over the world we will see that in most cases they die in a mysterious way, and would be seen not to be satisfied with the nature of the life they have lived – how they burn out the candle of their destiny pleasing the enemy. Some have traded their destiny for material wealth, as was the case with Esau. The Bible says that Esau was a cunning hunter, but he couldn't use his skill to secure his destiny. Though the case of Esau is adjudged as the will of God, we would notice that many of us have been duped in like manner. Our destiny is like a fuel in a can, which would be burnt to produce results – driving a car, used on our generators, etc. This same fuel can be exploded by an enemy and wasted.

- Destiny is made beautiful by the anointing. The anointing helps us to explore our purpose on Earth; to see what opportunities lies in wait for us to excel in life.

CHAPTER TWO

- Our parents and society influences our destiny, but we can retrace back the path that leads to it.

- As the years grow old, so also our destiny is drawing close to its termination.

- Sustaining our destiny is about discovering the unknown through the known. This is the reason why we must be willing to seek the knowledge of the Lord early enough, in our lives.

- Our destiny can be restored as long as we are willing to undergo processes put in place by the Lord, the opportunities He brings across us to transform us. This implies that we must have learned to plan our lives and live every second achieving the plan. Once you can plan your life, it would become your destiny in your palm.

- If we believe that destiny is about achieving set goals in life, then we will also believe that destiny can be manipulated and changed. This has happened severally in Africa, where a child destined with great success is seen suffering after his/her destiny has been swapped with another child. This fact will make many of us return to God to really ask what is indeed wrong with us and why it seems that things are not working the way they ought to, even after we have given our lives to Christ. It is what you know you pray about. It is what you pray about that the Angels take to God, and is there answered.

- Destiny can be delayed by deceit. This implies that the more we find ourselves in the midst of deceitful tongues, the more we find it difficult to fulfil our destiny.

- Destiny can be spoken to. This is the premise on which destinies can be manipulated, and also could be restored. What we confess with our mouths, and what people wish us, have a way of influencing our destiny. This is why the Lord says in Deuteronomy 28:6: *Blessed shalt thou be when thou comest in, and blessed shalt thou be when thou goest out.* We go out daily to fulfill our destiny, and as the days pass we are coming close to our destination in life. This is also the reason why we would receive a word from the Lord to transform our lives. As we understand this, we would then understand why we are admonished to avoid evil communication, and to flee from every appearance of evil. Learn to say good things about your life and your destiny. Wish yourself a good life and say good things concerning the future – yours, and those of others.

CHAPTER TWO

- The Oracle we receive from the Altar of the Lord is a destiny path tracer – meaning that no sensible believer would live without an Altar of the Lord where he submits to and would worship the Lord there.

- Patience helps us to achieve our destiny. This is why the Lord says, Luke 21:19: *In your patience possess ye your souls*. Once we possess our souls, we become in charge of what happens to us, and in no time we have arrived at our destination.

- Destiny involves vision. This is why we must see our destiny on time. Joseph saw his destiny on time, and the Lord led him there. Even in the midst of temptation, he kept himself from sin. If we see our destiny on time, we won't want anything that will stop us from achieving it. Once this happens, we will see that our destiny is intact and secured from satanic infiltrations as a child protected in its mother's womb. There are so many forces ganging up against our destiny – a fact we must know.

- Our destiny speaks in our heart, which means that if we can befriend our hearts, we would mind what we sow inside, so that our destiny is pure from pollution.

CHAPTER TWO

- Our destiny could be hidden in our names. We have seen several instances in the Bible of how names affected the lives people lived. We would also see God changing Abram to Abraham, Sarai to Sarah, and Jesus changing Simon to Peter. The later names hold more promising destinies than the earlier ones. Jabez prayed not to cause pain because his name meant sorrow, and we are told God answered his prayer – 1 Chronicles 4:9-10. If you are experiencing dissatisfaction in life and what you are passing through is an interpretation of your name, please meet the Lord for a new name.

- We are all children of destiny. On a day to day basis, ensure that your daily destinations takes you close to your final destination in life, to enable you to live a fulfilling destiny. If this weren't important, God wouldn't send Jesus to rescue the world.

- Put your destiny on the drive. Activate it. See it ahead of you and avoid destiny murderers. Even as Pharaoh and Herod physically murdered young children to prevent the work of the Lord, so we have spiritual Pharaohs and Herods working against your purpose in life. But if you can see it, you can walk into it and achieve it. The devil has launched a mass attack on the destiny of many, but few are yet to walk into the path that leads to life – Matthew 7:14.

- Since our reward in heaven is determined by the extent to which we actualized our destiny, the onus is upon us to ensure that we diligently fulfil our course on Earth. There is so much within our control.

- When we negatively affect others' destinies, we are held responsible and judged accordingly – Matthew 18:7. This implies that we have to be careful how we advise people, and how our lives affect them. Many will be damned because of the way their lives have affected people negatively and led them into eternal destruction.

- The devil does not have information about our destinies. We usually give it out to him without him requesting for it. For instance the devil wasn't with God when Jeremiah was being formed in his mothers womb, so how will he know about him? It was the Lord that said he knew Jeremiah in the preconceive state (Jeremiah 1:5).

- If we fail to complete our tasks, God will definitely get another to complete it. We are told that the word of the Lord does not return void – Isaiah 55:11: *So shall my word be that goeth forth out of my mouth: it shall not return unto me void, but it shall accomplish that which I please, and it shall prosper in the thing whereto I sent it.* And He will use humans to achieve each of the word He has spoken. Many of us have been stripped of our tasks before the Lord – Matthew 13:12. And since our tasks are linked to our destinies, it shows that many people will not fulfil their destinies.

CHAPTER THREE

SAVED TO SAVE OTHERS

A key verse of the Bible about what the Lord expects of us is seen in Luke 22:31-32: *And the Lord said, Simon, Simon, behold, Satan hath desired to have you, that he may sift you as wheat: But I have prayed for thee, that thy faith fail not: and when thou art converted, strengthen thy brethren.* We are saved so that we can render assistance to others. Meaning further, that we are in this world to fulfil one task or the other. As least, it is becoming clearer now that we are not created for ourselves only. Indeed we are admonished to love our neighbours as we love ourselves. We are a source of blessings to others; through us, the Lord can lift up others: Genesis 12:3: *And I will bless them that bless thee ... in thee shall all families of the earth be blessed.* The precondition there is that they would first bless us – how will people bless you when you have not offered them something of high value? It is only after you have done your best in trying to lift them up, and they refuse and instead start cursing you that the Lord will intervene - *and curse him that curseth thee.*

God fixes people in positions of trust when they have what it takes to sustain such a position. Abraham feared God and was ready to sacrifice his only son. Joseph had respect for God, in that he refused the enticement that adultery pushed before him. Daniel feared God, and refused to eat the king's delicacies. Esther was not carried away as queen but used her position to deliver the children of the Lord. God is waiting for the testimony of others through your act – Matthew 5:16. So we would say that the Bible is right when it says that the fear of the Lord is the beginning of wisdom (Proverbs 9:10). When we begin to fear God we will begin to ask Him what is His will, and we will learn His ways and follow His bidding. One clear fact is that the path that leads to life is narrow, and only few find it – Matthew 7:14. And so once we find this path, we shouldn't hesitate to help others discover it. Many would not want to pass through this same narrow path, because it is a path that requires

CHAPTER THREE

lots of patience, learning and walking on new paths of spiritual discovery and reality. As we learn of what is new, we will see a better clue to understanding what is old. As Jesus would say, He came to fulfil the law.

The New Testament beautified the purpose of the Old Testament. Again, the reality of life's pursuits is not about what we diagnose as the solution to the problems of life, but in the way we understand what we are going through presently and how it fits into the big picture of what God intends to do through us.

The question now is – are you saved? If it is true that we can confirm that we are saved from the worries of life, can we adjudge the same to be true for others who we believe share a common faith with us? Certainly this may not be true. Opinion has it severally that people often digress away from the path of life once they can perceive that they are no longer under the watchful eyes of the one they see as their mentors. And with this sort of life, there is every tendency that there would be ups and downs in people's lives. These ups and downs, occasioned by people's inability to subjugate their interior desires for the cuisines of world pleasure, envelop our thought processes and would be seen as the reason why many have forced themselves into accepting all manner of lifestyles that make them fit into certain circles. Is this what God will accept?

Our Lord Jesus lived a life of sanctification to be able to save others. He pointed everyone around Him to the Father – John 17:4: *I have glorified thee on the earth: I have finished the work which thou gavest me to do.* In His prayers before the Lord, He gave us the clue to what made Him to succeed in His ministry – John 17:19: *And for their sakes I sanctify myself, that they also might be sanctified through the truth.* On another occasion we would learn that He is meek and lowly in character – Matthew 11:29. Explaining this in layman's language so that we may understand what it takes to save others and help them to do the will of God, Saint Paul says (1 Corinthians 9:22-23): *To the weak became I as weak, that I might gain the weak: I am made all things to all men, that I might by all means save some. And this I do for the gospel's sake, that I might be partaker thereof with you.* This paints a picture of humble living. When we identify with the predicaments of others, and they see us as providing solutions to their problems, they will yield their strength into our hands, and would ask us to lead them.

This often turns out to be worship, as long as they can connect their solutions to you, until they find someone who gives them more than what you can provide for them. This is a misrepresentation of the intention of God, when he admonished us to save others. To put the lines straight, the Lord streamlined the help that we all need, and that wouldn't include the provision of food, clothing, what to drink, etc. – Matthew 6:25: *Therefore I say unto you, Take no thought for your life, what ye shall eat, or what ye shall drink; nor yet for your body, what ye shall put on. Is not the life more than meat, and the body than raiment.* But first desire to seek after Him, though this seems a difficult task when many who come to God only need a miracle to correct their long years of mistakes and misfortune.

We will see that Jesus said that His sheep hear His voice and come to Him. Anyone who would refuse to come to the Lord is not called by His name. It is the desire of the Lord that all would be saved – Acts 15:17: *That the residue of men might seek after the Lord, and all the Gentiles, upon whom my name is called, saith the Lord, who doeth all these things.* We would now break this down to our individual responsibility before the Lord –

the key words there are *might seek after the Lord.* We have no duty on Earth other than to seek after the Lord. Those who are called by the name of the Lord look for Him. These are they who have the mark of the Lord in their forehead right from birth. What will the Lord do when we seek after Him? He will teach us His ways – Isaiah 2:3. What then are the ways of the Lord that we have to lead others to? Jesus called this 'Truth.' What then is Truth? This was the same question Pilate asked Jesus (John 18:38), only he didn't wait to receive the answer from Jesus. This is how many of us, having come in contact with Lord, are often carried away from hearing the Truth. With time we may discover that all that we hear and live with are lies, fabricated by the haters of God, who only use His name to enrich their bank accounts.

It is often a difficult task to follow the bidding of the Lord. Jesus once prayed that the cup should pass over Him if it pleases God – Luke 22:42. He even encouraged the disciples to follow Him with the sword for protection, and they were able to get two swords (Luke 22:38), but we would see later that He rebuked them for using the sword as defence. This is how it is when we yield to the will of God – Matthew 26:52.

CHAPTER THREE

But will the Lord accept our act of repenting and backsliding at will? Our act of evangelism is only appreciated when we can successfully lead a soul to Christ. Heaven rejoices when the soul makes heaven at the end of the day. Many see soul winning as just ministering to people about Christ and following up until they begin to attend the church; it is more than this. The soul must become a soul winner, with the aim of leading them into heaven. This means the message of salvation should not be painted to attract the multitude, but to focus on the truth that will set everyone free, and to minister this wherever we go. As we continually do this, we will see the seed growing in the hearts of whomever we had planted it into. This is why the drive for carnal wealth will not take anyone anywhere near the Kingdom of God.

CHAPTER FOUR

NOW IS THE HOUR!

Severally Jesus made reference to the urgency of the work before us – as we are born on the face of this Earth to execute the will of God:

John 4:23: *But the hour cometh, and now is, when the true worshippers shall worship the Father in spirit and in truth: for the Father seeketh such to worship him.* We are born to join a congregation of worshippers (Psalm 42:4), to worship the Lord. We would see the urgency here - *the hour cometh, and now is.* This is the beginning of the fulfilment of our destiny on Earth. And we would see a reason for dedicating a child to the Lord, and thereafter bringing the child up in the way of the Lord, so that when the child grows old, he/she will not depart from it.

John 5:25: *Verily, verily, I say unto you, The hour is coming, and now is, when the dead shall hear the voice* *of the Son of God: and they that hear shall live.* Our destiny would involve a hearing process – that even the dead shall be raised to life. Who will He speak through? This is where you come in – representing the will of God on Earth. We would see the desire of heaven to bring succour into the hearts of those that mourn. Are you willing to be a part of this heavenly call, to put smiles on the faces of others? If yes, then you have a destiny to fulfil.

John 12:35-36: *Yet a little while is the light with you. Walk while ye have the light, lest darkness come upon you: for he that walketh in darkness knoweth not whither he goeth. While ye have light, believe in the light, that ye may be the children of light.* The urgent need to seek the way of the Lord, and do His will should be the utmost desire of everyone.

Luke 12:33-25: *Sell that ye have, and give alms; provide yourselves bags which wax not old, a treasure in the heavens that faileth not, where no thief approacheth, neither moth corrupteth. For where your treasure is, there will your heart be also. Let your loins be girded about, and your lights burning.* Implying that nothing should take our attention from fulfilling our destiny in the Lord. What is required of us is also captured here - *Let your loins be* *girded about, and your lights burning.* This means that we should be steadfast, and fully dedicated to the call of destiny. Many of us have been wasting time playing around like a child who is on an errand under oath yet decides to keep his father waiting in vain, while he plays around with his friends along the way.

We are informed of a spiritual secret in Psalm 58:3: *The wicked are estranged from the womb: they go astray as soon as they be born, speaking lies* – that once the wicked is born, the souls sent into the world by the devil start to execute their destiny for the world to feel their terror. If this is the case, why can't we do likewise, starting to execute our own destiny from birth? Working on the Lord's side is somewhat different, because it demands that we become pure and sanctified with His word before we can start to function in our calling – because all have sinned and come short of the glory that was given to us from the beginning, when Christ lighted us to come into the world.

Now that we know that we are saved to save others, we would now see in what manner we should carry out our task before the Lord. And we would know this from the way we expect our prayers to be answered by God.

CHAPTER FOUR

We have always wanted a miracle. This is why the Lord even says that the time is now – while it is yet day. The preacher says it must be in the days of your youth (Ecclesiastes 12:1). The Lord reminded Joshua of his task and what he needed to succeed – Joshua 1:6: *Be strong and of a good courage: for unto this people shalt thou divide for an inheritance the land, which I sware unto their fathers to give them.* This was Joshua's destiny before the Lord.

How can we achieve this? John 1:9 says: *That was the true Light, which lighteth every man that cometh into the world,* and this gives us a clue of what happens when we are on our way to execute the will of God on Earth as ordained by God. Our soul receives the light of God, and it is this light that helps us to trace our way back to the Lord. We are born to do the will of God, but the moment we step into this world, we are influenced by two other wishes: our own carnal wish and the wish of the environment where we are born. To make things more complex, the wish of the environment even goes further, to include the wish of our parents, the wish of our siblings, the wish of our parents' families, the wish of others, the wish of our nation, that of our continent and the wish of the world as a whole. From what we try to analyse above, we would see that the wish of the environment commands more burden upon us than that of God and ours. If we then yield to the will of God alone, we would see that within us we would have peace since our mind becomes united with the purpose of heaven. But the obvious truth is that the wishes of the environment we find ourselves will cause turbulence around us physically, and we may often be seen as being insensitive to the plight of society. If society wants to carry out the wish of God, from our immediate families to the outside world, we will see a unification of wishes, and the world will be at peace. This is the reason why we preach the gospel to each and everyone so that their hearts will begin to beat with the thoughts of the Kingdom of God. If this is the case, we will all with time have no individual destiny to fulfil, but we will act as Angels of God here on Earth, exercising His will here. This is the ultimate wish of God for our Earth.

We must at this juncture start to understand that we really don't have a life of our own, though the Lord has given us the free will to choose what life we want to live. He does this out of love, and this is the reason we have so much Earth life to live – if we all were to do the will of God from the day we were born, we wouldn't need to live a hundred years or so, though our early years on Earth are expected to be spent gathering information as we investigate all that is happening on Earth. This is to enable us to compare the ideal heavenly wish for the Earth with the reality on ground. Some of us get our facts together on time and would present our findings before the Lord as we complain to restore. Many would be employed immediately in an existing rescue team – the church with a specific name, mission statement and vision.

Sometimes, because of the diverse nature of the problem on the ground, and the need for the Lord to evolve new strategies but with the same vision, he would constitute some other rescue teams with a leader. He would appoint and then deploy more hands to assist him – this is how a church is born. In all these, we are born to do exploits for the Lord. First we must note that it would really be of no value to God if we were sent down to Earth only to experience pain all the days of our lives, as many scripture verses would testify.

CHAPTER FIVE

BORN TO EXPERIENCE FAVOUR

We are told that Jesus succeeded because He had the Holy Spirit, Wisdom and Grace – Luke 2:40: *And the child grew, and waxed strong in spirit, filled with wisdom: and the grace of God was upon him,* and with this *He was in favour with God and man* – Luke 2:52. The difference between the anointing upon Jesus and John was in the fact that John the Baptist only had the Spirit – Luke 1:80: *And the child grew, and waxed strong in spirit, and was in the deserts till the day of his shewing unto Israel.* And because of this extra anointing upon Jesus. Wisdom and Grace, John understood that Jesus …*shall baptize you in the Holy Spirit and in fire: whose fan is in his hand, and he will thoroughly cleanse his threshing-floor; and he will gather his wheat into the garner, but the chaff he will burn*

CHAPTER FIVE

up with unquenchable fire – Matthew 3:11-12. It was therefore common sense that Jesus would increase while John would decrease – John 3:30-31: *He must increase, but I must decrease. He that cometh from above is above all: he that is of the earth is earthly, and speaketh of the earth: he that cometh from heaven is above all.* Every wise one who intends to fulfil his destiny in Jesus must look unto heaven, from where his/her help would come. Jesus is the only Master. Even in His first coming, we saw in the Bible references where he would command His disciples to instruct the head of a household that the master want to use his house, and there was no argument to this fact – Matthew 26:18: *And he said, Go into the city to such a man, and say unto him, The Master saith, My time is at hand; I will keep the passover at thy house with my disciples.* When the Master lives in you, no one can deny you anything, because you will be talking with the voice and authority of the master.

No one succeeds without experiencing favour. Jesus achieved because He found favour with God and men – Luke 2:52: *And Jesus increased in wisdom and stature, and in favour with God and man.* It was His destiny as the Son of God to experience favour. And so, if we have truly yielded to the will of God, we will in like manner experience even greater favour from God and men because Jesus is on the throne, in heaven. But before we continue we would see what Jesus came to do, from where we would be also discovering our own destiny – Luke 3:5-6: *Every valley shall be filled, and every mountain and hill shall be brought low; and the crooked shall be made straight, and the rough ways shall be made smooth; And all flesh shall see the salvation of God (a confirmation of Isaiah 40:4)*. The Lord expects that each one of us would fit into an aspect of this great call to restore the Earth. The deprived and poor here referred to as the valley shall be exalted. The wicked and oppressors of humanity, here referred to as mountain and hill, shall be brought low. All deceit shall be exposed, hidden wisdom shall be revealed, and the power of God will fill the Earth. Are you seeing your destiny revealed here? But to achieve this, you need favour from God and men.

Now lets look at some of the favour Jesus had while on Earth:

From God: several verses of the Bible testify to this fact:

- Matthew 3:16,17: *And Jesus, when he was baptized, went up straightway out of the water: and, lo, the heavens were opened unto him, and he saw the Spirit of God descending like a dove, and lighting upon him: And lo a voice from heaven, saying, This is my beloved Son, in whom I am well pleased.* God announced Jesus right before the face of everyone there present. This is how favour works – if we yield to His will, He will be the one to announce us. Many of us struggle to make ends meet, even in our careers and businesses, and it seem as if things are not working as we expect. God can still announce us if we care to stick to His bidding.

- John 11:41: *And Jesus lifted up his eyes, and said, Father, I thank thee that thou hast heard me. And I knew that thou hearest me always.* This is a statement of affirmation of an existing relationship built on trust.

Now we would see evidence of Jesus finding favour with men:

From men: below are some Bible verses to prove that Jesus found favour with men:

- **John 3:1-2:** *There was a man of the Pharisees, named Nicodemus, a ruler of the Jews: The same came to Jesus by night, and said unto him, Rabbi, we know that thou art a teacher come from God: for no man can do these miracles that thou doest, except*

God be with him. The high in class came to meet Him secretly because of the works of God in His life. This is why I frown against people running after help and those in power. When the favour of God is upon you, people – low and high will look for you, to receive the wisdom you have.

- **Matthew 2:14:** *And as he passed by, he saw Levi the son of Alphaeus sitting at the receipt of custom, and said unto him, Follow me. And he arose and followed him.* This is Levi, later called Matthew, working under the authority of the government –more like a customs officer at duty, following Jesus as He beckoned to him. Does this paint a picture of our regard and respect? If we tell people to follow us to do the work of the Lord and they are not responding, it shows that we don't have the favour of God yet. The favour of God attracts the favour of men.

- **Matthew 21:2:** *Saying unto them, Go into the village over against you, and straightway ye shall find an ass tied, and a colt with her: loose them, and bring them unto me. And if any man say ought unto you, ye shall say, The Lord hath need of them; and straightway he will send them.* Jesus was so confident

CHAPTER FIVE

that any owner of a donkey would send it at His request. He is the master and cannot be denied anything. Can we see favour in display here. Yes, of course! We are told later (verses 6-8)- *And the disciples went, and did as Jesus commanded them, And brought the ass, and the colt, and put on them their clothes, and they set him thereon. And a very great multitude spread their garments in the way; others cut down branches from the trees, and strawed them in the way.* He was honoured thereafter with a hosanna song to the extent that people started asking who He was (verse 10) - *And when he was come into Jerusalem, all the city was moved, saying, Who is this?* It is this favour that the Lord has given to you, and the world will have no choice but to celebrate the light of the Lord shining upon you. When a light falls on an object it does two things – it is reflected and also refracted. The reflected light creates a shining luminous spark of brightness; this is what causes the physical attraction. The refracted light creates warmth within and fills our heart with the message born by the light, and when people come to us as a result of the attraction created by the reflected light, we would speak to them with the refracted light, thus releasing the warmth in our hearts to them – this warmth soon envelops them and they also will feel the effect of the light that is reflecting from our faces and lives in us.

- **Luke 23:11:** *And Herod with his men of war set him at nought, and mocked him, and **arrayed him in a gorgeous robe,** and sent him again to Pilate.* Even from Herod, after he and his men had mocked Him, Jesus was still clothed with a gorgeous robe.

What then is favour? The Oxford Dictionary of English defines 'favour' as; *'overgenerous preferential treatment, an act of kindness beyond what is due or usual.'*

What could this definition represent? Firstly, from God, we have salvation and our sins are wiped away the moment we confess Jesus as our Lord and saviour. Again, we have the sun shining and the rains falling on both the good and the evil, as the show of His love towards mankind. When the world had written us off, then we were favoured by God with a job, husband, wife, children, home, etc. From humans, we would see that sometimes we are given opportunities that we didn't expect. Someone could pay our school fees or present a gift on honour to us when it is obvious that we didn't merit such

CHAPTER FIVE

by all available standard of weighting. You will understand the works of God in your life better when you have lost all hope, and there before you came your help.

Now that we understand what favour is all about, I would encourage you to also write out the favours you have received from God and from men. It is only when we can list these out that we would know how far we have impacted the world, because we need the favour of God to impact lives, and that would automatically bring the favour from men. We shouldn't see the achievements that we have achieved on Earth through the act of swindling others as a feat of favour from God. And we shouldn't see opportunities we have from men through living a life of deceit as an act of favour from men. Our greatness comes from our teaching and doing the will of God – Matthew 5:19: ... *but whosoever shall do and teach them, the same shall be called great in the kingdom of heaven.*

The only thing that can separate you from the love of God is sin, just as it did Adam. We are going to see how we can avoid sin, and be perfect before God (Philippians 2:15). In psalm 51:10, David begged God to renew his inner mind, who is the spirit within him. This is the starting point. We need to pray like David all the time so that God can have mercy upon us.

CHAPTER FIVE

The following are needed to remain faithful:

- There shall be no deceit in your heart – John 1:47
- Do not forsake God – Jeremiah 17:13, because He is your strength and salvation
- Learn to forgive – Matthew 5:38-41

CHAPTER SIX

STRIVE TO LIVE YOUR DESTINY IN THE LORD

Disability is the inability to discover one's abilities. Saint Paul confirmed, in Philippians 4:13, that he could do all things because he had the backing of the spiritual – the Christ! Those who bear the hardship of life by night had designed their bearings of success before it was noon. If we must be patient as the vulture, then we should be ready to perch on refuse dumps because our success depends on how we are able to turn waste into wealth. We are encouraged with the fact that *with God all things are possible* – Mark 10:27.

A man once had a dream and he told his friend, who said he had likewise had a similar dream. They agreed to tell their wives. Their wives told each of their friends, and

CHAPTER SIX

those equally told their husbands. The dream finally fell into the ears of a dumb man. The dumb man couldn't reveal it to anyone, so he decided to put it in writing. The more he wrote it out, the more the dream was bringing meaning to him. Startled by what the dream had turned out to be in his mind, and perceiving that the king of the land would be interested in it, he wrote to the king that he had a revelation to share with him. Quickly the king sent for him, because at that time, the land was experiencing many of issues. When he got to the palace, he was ushered in. When he got to the king, he motioned to them with his hand that he was dumb.

Astonished, the king asked how he would reveal the vision. The dumb man presented the paper where he had drafted the vision. He had even explained, in wisdom, how the dream would be materialised to add value to the kingdom. The king was so pleased, and invited every member of his cabinet. The dumb man was appointed as the executor of the vision and provided with an entourage that would follow him about as he ministered hope into the hearts of every citizen in the land, making provisions for their needs. There was great joy in the land. The king offered him his daughter as a wife. The

CHAPTER SIX

fame of the kingdom soon became known all over the nations.

The two friends who had the dream soon heard of it and discovered that every bit of what was now in place in the physical world was exactly what they had seen in their dreams. They inquired how they could see the king, so that the king would assist them to also put things right in their own land. The king led them to the dumb man. The man narrated how he had got the dream on to paper and how he had prayed for the Lord to explain the meaning of the dream to him. One thing was sure in their hearts when they heard the story.

Both returned home to ask their wives if they had told anybody the dream, and they admitted that they had. On tracing the route the information had followed, they discovered that the dumb man was a beggar who usually sat at the gate of one of those who had received the dream, and had honestly cast it out as a mere dream.

Many of us only see our destinies in our dreams and fail to put it in the practice in the real world. What we give attention to is what takes the centre of our emotions. It is what we direct our emotions at that becomes the resource that we draw from to make a living.

CHAPTER SIX

Many of us have soaked our emotions in jealousy and have consistently drawn hatred from those of whom we are jealous. Many of us dismiss dreams immediately we wake up. I don't do that - I rather ask the Lord to reveal the secret meaning behind the dream to me. Pharaoh and Nebuchadnezzar didn't dismiss their dreams, horrible as they were. They rather sought help, and the Lord sent them help, and the land reaped the benefit of the dream. We were told how these kings had sleepless nights until they had the mysterious dreams resolved.

How can we achieve our destiny in the Lord? Through enrolling under His tutelage. The Bible encouraged us thus - *Receive my instruction, and not silver; and knowledge rather than choice gold. For wisdom is better than rubies; and all the things that may be desired are not to be compared to it* – Proverbs 8:10-11. Why this advice? It is because life becomes easy and *plain to him that understandeth, and right to them that find knowledge* (Proverbs 8:9). The drive for materialism is making it difficult for many to fulfil their destiny. And in the midst of these quests, we are thrown into a sea of complaints, backbiting, gossiping, jealousy, etc.

When we surrender unto the bidding of the Holy

CHAPTER SIX

Spirit, the Lord empowers us, and beautifies us in like manner. If there is anything I have come to realise about fulfilling my destiny in the Lord, it is His ever-present hand of help. He even goes to the extent of making us presentable, so that we are not denied anything. In Isaiah 61:6, we are promised the wealth of the Gentiles, provided we would become priests and servants unto Him: *But ye shall be named the Priests of the Lord: men shall call you the Ministers of our God: ye shall eat the riches of the Gentiles, and in their glory shall ye boast yourselves.* This verse talks of people who have a destiny of 'Priesthood' and 'Minister' to fulfil before the Lord.

Now let's look at those under the covenant of God in Ezekiel 16:9-14:

Then washed I thee with water; yea, I throughly washed away thy blood from thee, and I anointed thee with oil. I clothed thee also with broidered work, and shod thee with badgers 'skin, and I girded thee about with fine linen, and I covered thee with silk. I decked thee also with ornaments, and I put bracelets upon thy hands, and a chain on thy neck. And I put a jewel on thy forehead, and earrings in thine ears, and a beautiful crown upon thine head. Thus wast thou decked with gold and silver; and thy raiment was of fine linen, and silk, and broidered work; thou didst eat fine flour, and honey, and oil: and thou wast exceeding beautiful, and thou didst prosper into a kingdom. And thy renown went forth among the heathen for thy beauty: for it was perfect through my comeliness, which I had put upon thee, saith the Lord God

From this Bible extract, we would see the following as what the Lord will do for anyone who submits under His bidding:

- The Lord first washes away the blood of sins from them and then anoints them with oil. This oil is also called the oil of gladness – Psalm 45:7: *Thou lovest righteousness, and hatest wickedness: therefore God, thy God, hath anointed thee with the oil of gladness above thy fellows.* This oil sets them above others (Deuteronomy 28:13).

- He clothes them in royalty and all manner of ornaments to make them attractive. All these are spiritual beautification put in place for all those who will indeed follow the Lord.

- This process led them into belonging into a kingdom where they would enjoy their own freedom of rule, without interference from the outside, which would carry away their wealth.

CHAPTER SIX

How then can one strive to fulfil one's destiny? It must be 'purpose-driven'. It must be 'service to the people' oriented. We must have a balanced approach to issues as they evolve daily, and we are opportune to come across them. We must not take the judge's stance and condemn others outright, as Jesus warned in Matthew 7:1: *Judge not, that ye be not judged.* We shouldn't be seen as trying to pull down what God is building. And we mustn't be seen in the company of evildoers – gossips, susurrates, blackmailers, seducers, etc. All these are acts of destiny destruction. Jesus called them heart pollutants – Mark 7:21: *For from within, out of the heart of men, proceed evil thoughts, adulteries, fornications, murders, Thefts, covetousness, wickedness, deceit, lasciviousness, an evil eye, blasphemy, pride, foolishness: All these evil things come from within, and defile the man.* Whatever has the power to defile also has the power to destroy destiny. As we strive to fulfil our destiny in the Lord, because He is the only one with the answer to what will happen to us tomorrow, our observance of His code of conduct, in His vineyard, is all we need to move forward.

We are told the story in the Bible of Solomon, who was faced with the challenges of succeeding as a king.

CHAPTER SIX

He went to God and prayed to the Lord to give him wisdom.

In the discussion that follows we would be seeing some aspects of the destiny we have to fulfil.

- **Fulfilling the destiny in your name:** Ask for any special prayer that was prayed the day you were named and during your dedication to God. Ask to know also what were the expectations of your parents as they prayed to have a child, and you finally became that answer. My mother always says of me that an angel visited her, and had come to bring a child unto her. I was christened 'Oghenethoja,' meaning 'God is help', 'God is salvation' or 'God is peace.' So it wouldn't be out of place if I bear the message of hope to people in need and in distress. Let's take the name 'Desire,' for instance; it would be obvious that the parents see the child as one who will fulfil their desire of joy and peace. And so, any time the child is seen, what will come to people's mind is that the child is the answer to the desire they had prayed for. Now if the one named 'Desire' is unable to provide the answer wherever he/she is, it shows that the name is not working as intended yet. My children answer names of prophetic symbolism – *Odeviano* (my name is announced), *Elomezino* (my glory has come), *Aghoghomena* (this is my joy), and *Ewevino* (laughter has increased).

- **Fulfilling the prophecy on your baptismal day:** On our baptismal day, we submitted to the will of God, and we were baptised in the name of the Father, the Son and the Holy Spirit. The day Jesus was baptised the heavens opened and a voice declared who Jesus is. Later, we would see that Jesus fulfilled the declaration upon Him – the Son of God, with whom God is well pleased.

- **Ask to know what happened when you were born:** What were the world events that happened when you were born? What is your family history? What happened in the environment where you were born? These are clues to what God expects from you. Let's take a look at the time Jesus was born – Luke 2:1-7: *And it came to pass in those days, that there went out a decree from Caesar Augustus, that all the world should be taxed ... And so it was, that, while they were there, the days were accomplished that she should be delivered. And she brought forth her firstborn son.* The whole world would be levied with a heavy burden under the imperial rule of injustice. It was a perfect time to give birth to the saviour of the world. And during His days we would see Him wining Matthew, a tax collector, and dining with Zacchaeus, another tax man, and finally he would be crucified by the Romans. This set in place the perfect scenery for a take-over of authority. We can see that today, the Romans have lost control of the world they once ruled over. The heavenly host praising with a song in verse 14 - *Glory to God in the highest, and on earth peace, good will toward men,* only confirmed this fact.

- **Know what odd events are happening around where you are living now.** The odd events happening around you now as you live also call for your attention. Remember God is seeking who will say *'restore'* – Isaiah 42:22. This is the reason you must be well informed of recent events. Spend some time listening to news and keeping abreast of world events. Moses wasn't comfortable with the sufferings of the children of Israel in Egypt. The future famine that was to visit the world in the days of Joseph set him on the pedestal of power to influence.

CHAPTER SEVEN

THE PLACE OF EDUCATION

What is education? I tend to go with the definition in the online Wikipedia, which states that 'Education in its general sense is a form of learning in which the knowledge, skills and habits of a group of people are transferred from one generation to the next through teaching, training, or research.[1]'

The purpose of education can be seen from Proverbs 1:2-4: *To know wisdom and instruction; to perceive the words of understanding; To receive the instruction of wisdom, justice, and judgment, and equity; To give subtilty to the simple, to the young man knowledge and discretion.*

We would now break down the key words from what we just read. Education involves:

1 - http://en.wikipedia.org/wiki/Education.

- Knowing wisdom and instruction, as they relate to our ability to provide solutions to problems on ground. This is why we have people trained in various professions and careers.

- Perceiving the words of understanding, enabling us to make right judgements, and streamlining our desires to favour only what we really need, rather than soaking our thoughts in matters of less importance.

- Receiving the instruction of wisdom, justice and judgment and equity. In line with the last discussed item, what we receive is what we become over time, and this has a way of affecting all that we do, and will happen to us.

- Giving farsightedness, knowledge and opportunity to different categories of people as they would need, to enable them to make the right choices in line amidst a plethora of opportunities.

We have both formal and informal education. Informal education does not follow a particular pattern, it comes as the day grows – it is the kind of training we get from our parents and those we see as mentors. Formal education, on the other hand, deals with structured learning, following what is usually called a syllabus, and at the end a certificate is usually awarded. Our ability to work in a team and see ourselves as part of the vision to put things in order wherever we are has a lot to do with what we learnt from both formal and informal education. Many times, people just pass through the learning process, with the learning affecting their lives. How often have we seen highly-trained professionals in society talking senselessly, especially when they have been brainwashed by induced religious beliefs?

Jesus says in Matthew 13:52: ...*Therefore every scribe who has been trained for the kingdom of heaven is like a master of a house, who brings out of his treasure what is new and what is old* (ESV). Training gives one authority to act in certain jurisdiction. It brings confidence and purpose. With these, we are definitely in charge.

Our day-to-day engagements involve meeting people and communicating with them. This explains why we need some form of training: understanding and using certain languages in speech and writing, studying the cultures and behaviours of people, understanding the subjects of science, taking a study in accounting principles and economics, presentations skills development, understanding the rules of engagement in certain instances, etc.

What will education do for us? We have a clue in Ecclesiastes 10:10: *If the iron be blunt, and he do not whet the edge, then must he put to more strength: but wisdom is profitable to direct.* Education is needed to sharpen our dull memories and intelligence. Education empowers us with wisdom, which we would use to direct our path in life and that of others. This is why the sought of education we receive is important, especially as we grow from being a child into adulthood. What differentiates people is the manner of education they had received. Education yields its value when we seek to use the wisdom we are going to gain to solving problems.

Education involves enrolling under the tutelage of a mentor. Jesus says – Luke 6:40: *…but everyone when he is fully trained will be like his teacher* (ESV). The verse we just read talks about one being fully trained to be able to attain a certain level of proficiency and the command of authority. This requires humility and patience on both sides – the mentor and the mentored. Jesus says that we have to learn of Him – Matthew 11:28. The absence of this is the reason many are unable to do the will of God – Luke 6:46: *And why call ye me, Lord, Lord, and do not the things which I say.*

Moses was trained in the learning of the Egyptian sages, and that qualified him as one who would become god to Pharaoh. Why? It is simple logic – Moses had what the magicians of Egypt had, he added what his in-law had, and how he met the Lord, who now gave him better understanding of what is right and wrong, and then empowered to put the enemy to flight.

When the Lord called me into His service, one morning I heard that I needed six years' training before I would begin to function, at least to a certain acceptable standard. If I had rejected that voice, I would have been seen today running from pillar to post seeking wisdom from men. But six years down the line, as I write this book, the thirteenth in six years, I can see my wisdom maturing, and it shows in the way I pray, praise, counsel, talk, etc. I used to be afraid of talking to people because I felt I could not quote the Bible verses, but that is gone. I have had the opportunity of ministering to a people who had heard great preachers and I would get their commendation – 'wow, this was spirit enriching.' When

CHAPTER SEVEN

I started singing, many advised me to let it go, that I wasn't gifted to sing. The same people are singing a different song about me today – I would hear them say, 'that was lovely.' What did I do? I simply went inside to pray for strength and I bought books, browsed the Internet, listened to others, and learnt.

One great way to learn is studying the Bible. The power of the word of God is inestimable. This is why the translators of the King James Bible, in 1611, wrote: *God's sacred Word . . . is that inestimable treasure that excelleth all the riches of the earth.* This is why we encourage people to use the Bible as a moral training syllabus. The Bible has the power of transforming us beyond our imagination. In the Bible lie the clues to our paths in life – the paths to our destination.

In general terms, our learning should be focused on the need at the time. The education we receive should help us to offer solutions to those in need, and then to society. For instance, the world is in need of teachers who would teach the Word of God with great spiritual insight. If you know you have this call, nothing stops you, after praying for the leading of the Lord, from submitting to the teaching of an anointed teacher. As you hear him teach, there is a spirit that will spring forth from the inside, and before you know it, you are already getting deep spiritual Rhema.

One key to having a great educational experience is sensing the area of need for improvement in your life – in your character, behaviour, specific knowledge, etc. Once this is identified, the next stage would be to identify the trainer who understands what you need. Then you must have a generous heart to be able to give to your trainer – this makes him reveal more professional secrets to you, and it will make him go out of his casual way to seek the knowledge that will help empower you. Jesus had no vineyard of his own while He was on earth. How did He feed? He wasn't employed in a government or public service, yet He was well clothed. People who had come to hear Him, and to whom He might have been of help in spiritual matters, provided for His upkeep. If you can take care of your teacher, you will receive more empowerment. This is the reason we pay tuition fees at school.

The education we receive can only begin to bear fruits in our lives when we 'Live by it,' by **Teaching it**, **Talking it**, and **Rehearsing it** (Teach, Talk, Rehearse (TTR)), to the observation of others – Deuteronomy 6:6-9: *And these* *words, which I command thee this day, shall be in thine heart: And thou shalt teach them diligently unto thy children, and shalt talk of them when thou sittest in thine house, and when thou walkest by the way, and when thou liest down, and when thou risest up. And thou shalt bind them for a sign upon thine hand, and they shall be as frontlets between thine eyes. And thou shalt write them upon the posts of thy house, and on thy gates.*

In other words, it must become a part and parcel of us. It must form the basis of the life we live daily. It should be like a vehicle that conveys us to wherever we want to be. Many times we may see people dropping their education at the gate of the institution, and would still be the same manner of person prior to receiving the specific education. Some people have been referred to as uneducated literate. They could read and write, but the behavioural value expected hasn't been learned. Education is profitable when we become what we have learned.

My advice is, get to the highest level of achievement in your chosen path of career, if that is what is needed to achieve a mark of honour on the path of your destiny. Fulfil all spiritual obligations before the Lord by growing spiritually to a level of immortal spiritual consciousness where you will begin to hear a spiritual voice. Participate in realistic spiritual exercises of fasting and prayers. Many have complained of undergoing spiritual exercises, and their lives seems to be in the same unpleasant condition. All I have to say is that when we engage in realistic spiritual exercises we will get results, because we are doing it in line with the principles and precepts of God. We can't have results when we want to have our way without considering the will of God at the material time. This is why it is good to hear from God before embarking on any fasting and prayer exercises, so that you will be focused on achieving the will of God for you.

CHAPTER EIGHT

HEAVEN'S GATE BECKONS - HELL'S GATE OPENS

A young man set out on a life journey which he must undertake once in his lifetime. The expedition involves taking a ride on a boat across a river to a land where a treasure is kept waiting for him in the hand of an old man. This old man is called 'The Ancient of Days.' There are however some instructions that he must adhere to. The land where the treasure is hidden does not accept the dead – meaning no dead body may be buried there; the entire land would be defiled if this happened. The river is sacred and would also be defiled if a dead body is thrown in it or drowns in it. The treasure cannot be kept in the same boat, house or within the vicinity of the

CHAPTER EIGHT

dead as this will defile the treasure and make it valueless. Failure to adhere to these would result in fatal consequences including death, desolation in the land, deprivation, etc.

He was given a final instruction not to change the garment he put on at the beginning of the journey until he got the treasure and returned to his land. The journey would take him as long as it took him to ride across the river, get the treasure and ride back – it is within his control, within his ability and strength.

The young man set out one early morning with a friend, for he feared that he would be lonely, and was afraid of possible attack from other water users, animals etc. The water was rough for several days and the cold was getting a hold on them. He sailed for days and nights, and then months, and on the seventh month from the day he left his land, he arrived on the shore of the treasure land.

With joy he exclaimed – 'I am here at last.' Turning to embrace his friend, he discovered that his friend was dead. How and when he had died was unknown to him. As he tried to pull his dead friend out of the boat, he remembered the instructions he had been given at the beginning. The old man held out the treasure to him, but

CHAPTER EIGHT

he couldn't receive it because he had a dead friend to deal with. What would he do now?

It is a journey that must be taken once in a lifetime. Life is an individual race. The more we trust in the protection of others, the more we lose hold on our God-given treasure – our destiny. Life is full of instructions to adhere to, and our close ties with people may make it impossible for us to obey these instructions.

You may see that in Mark 10:29, Jesus says: *And Jesus answered and said, Verily I say unto you, There is no man that hath left house, or brethren, or sisters, or father, or mother, or wife, or children, or lands, for my sake, and the gospel's.* We would leave everything to chase this 'once-in-a-life-time' opportunity and the reward is seen in verse 30: *But he shall receive an hundredfold now in this time, houses, and brethren, and sisters, and mothers, and children, and lands, with persecutions; and in the world to come eternal life.* In verse 31, a very important lesson is drawn - *But many that are first shall be last; and the last first.* Just like our dear friend in the story we just read, his reliance on the arm of man to accompany him has rendered him the last. Someone has to take the dead body of his friend from him before he can proceed to

CHAPTER EIGHT

receive his treasure. He would have to wait for another who will take the journey and be compassionate enough to assist him, so that the two treasures can be kept in one boat, maybe his, while the dead rides on a separate boat with the owner. This again depends on trust, that is, if the other will trust him to leave his treasure in his hand. This assumes the two treasures would not be too heavy for a boat. This is how complex life becomes when we are afraid to take the journey of life alone, hoping that someone out there will provide protection and provision for us.

We may have heard the saying that 'destiny can be delayed but cannot be denied.' This is the premise on which I am taking this discussion. Though this is true, what I want us to ask ourselves is what role did we play to delay our destiny, and what role are we playing now to ensure it is not denied? One great source of help in this wise is what we just discussed in the last chapter – specific and need-tailored education.

Once the gate of heaven beckons to us, the gates of hell open as well.

We may take a lesson from Jesus' words to Peter, upon His confirmation that Peter was growing in spiritual knowledge and understanding – Matthew 16:18: *...and upon this rock I will build my church; and the gates of hell shall not prevail against it.* The gates of hell couldn't close against the knowledge Peter had gotten, which was what Jesus was waiting to see as a confirmation of who would lead His disciples and through whom the Holy Spirit would be ministered to many after He had left for Heaven. What was Peter's destiny? Christ had changed his name earlier – Mark 3:16: *And Simon he surnamed Peter.* This name means 'Rock,' so the Lord conferred on him this title finally after he had demonstrated the capacity to really become the foundation. And Jesus says the reason he could get that information was simply because the heavens opened for him – Matthew 16:17: *Blessed art thou, Simon Barjona: for flesh and blood hath not revealed it unto thee, but my Father which is in heaven.* You would see that when heaven's gate beckons, hell's gate opens. Peter's destiny was delayed until he got the approval of heaven.

How far are we helping ourselves to lift up the gates of hell standing against our destiny? Peter followed Jesus as one of the trusted three, learning the mysteries of the Kingdom of God. Are you in a hurry to get a miracle, then there is every tendency that your destiny will be

CHAPTER EIGHT

delayed? What you need is not the miracle per se, but the knowledge of the 'deep water.' This is the beauty of counsel as seen in Proverbs 20:5: *Counsel in the heart of man is like deep water; but a man of understanding will draw it out.* With the right counsel, you are on the track to a wisdom-enriched and fulfilling destiny.

A young man would stand in front of where he lived, daily waiting to hear news from everyone who had gone out trying to make a living. On this day, one came and told a story of his odd encounters and how the day had been a hectic one with no food to eat at the end of it. This young man only replied with the words – 'I said it.' Another came and told a story of how he narrowly escaped an accident on his way to work that morning. And the young man replied with the same words – 'I said it.' Soon, someone came with the story of how successful the day was and how he had been favoured by God, with so much for him to eat. This young man frowned and left the scene. He soon walked into a gathering of people who were narrating stories about themselves and others who hadn't been able to get the pieces of life together and were dissatisfied with life. The young man, on hearing this, exclaimed, 'I said it.'

Everyone turned towards him. On seeing that he now

had their attention, he told them: 'I have vowed not to go anywhere to make ends meet because I don't want to experience any of these disappointments.' Everyone there mocked him and laughed at him. Then one of them asked him a question – 'who will fend for you?' Looking into his eyes, the young man replied, 'the dead don't need food to live.'

On hearing this, all those who were gathered dispersed hurriedly to their various destinations. Now that they knew he wasn't a living figure but a dead man living among them, no one ever stopped to tell him what transpired in their lives daily.

After some days, they discovered that they no longer saw the young man at his usual spot. But what was now there was a signpost, which read – LIFE IS WHAT YOU MAKE OF IT. They had wasted their time complaining to someone who didn't have the solution to their problem; someone who was already dead and had no need for daily bread. This is what many of us do. We spend time narrating our odd experiences, wishing someone would hear our story and sympathise with us some day. Whatever transpired in the course of the day is dead and gone. Of what use is waking the dead when it would

CHAPTER EIGHT

only interfere with our plan for the other day? Our sorrows are dead. Our disappointments are dead. Our misfortunes are dead. The only thing alive now is the hour we have now. Take time to plan this hour and the next hour will open its door for you to come in.

I took a lesson from the encounter of Saint Paul some years ago and I vowed not to take notice of the scenes of disappointments staring at me – 2 Corinthians 12:7-9: *And lest I should be exalted above measure through the abundance of the revelations, there was given to me a thorn in the flesh, the messenger of Satan to buffet me, lest I should be exalted above measure. For this thing I besought the Lord thrice, that it might depart from me. And he said unto me, My grace is sufficient for thee: for my strength is made perfect in weakness.* Here we would see Paul begging God for a smooth ride through life and the only consolation he received from God was – 'continue to endure it all, because I am with you always.' How would you feel after you had come to the point of your rescue and were only told to wait for a time?

Three young men, Shadrach, Meshach and Abednego, were cast into the furnace to be burnt to death. And while there, the Lord came to join them. To them, the Lord had come to take them out – but lo! They stayed until the one who cast them in exclaimed and announced the presence of the Lord, and they were let loose. We are told they had challenged the king to his face and opted to be thrown into the burning fiery furnace, believing in their heart that God would deliver them – Daniel 3:17: *If it be so, our God whom we serve is able to deliver us from the burning fiery furnace, and he will deliver us out of thine hand, O king.* The men that took them in died of the flame from the fire, but these expeditors lived. Why were they calm in the midst of their ordeal? The Lord was there with them and as such the fire didn't had power to consume them – Daniel 3:27: *...upon whose bodies the fire had no power, nor was an hair of their head singed, neither were their coats changed, nor the smell of fire had passed on them.* Again we would see Daniel cast into the lion's den as a test of his will to stand on the side of the Lord, and he was protected and saved unhurt – Daniel 6:20-22: *And when he came to the den, he cried with a lamentable voice unto Daniel: and the king spake and said to Daniel, O Daniel, servant of the living God, is thy God, whom thou servest continually, able to deliver thee from the lions?*

CHAPTER EIGHT

Then said Daniel unto the king, O king, live for ever. My God hath sent his angel, and hath shut the lions 'mouths, that they have not hurt me: forasmuch as before him innocency was found in me; and also before thee, O king, have I done no hurt.

What is key in what we just read is the fact that Daniel stood on the side of God, no matter the temptations and trials of faith, that tend to hinder him from actualising his destiny to serve the Lord.

Is there any circumstance intimidating you right now and trying to make you sweep your faith and destiny under the carpet? Remember, you are not the only one in this race – many of those smiling faces you see out there are passing through the worst situations in life, but they are counting it all joy to stay alive and please the Lord. Rest assured that even as you step out tomorrow there will be trials to overcome, but the Bible says (Matthew 6:25): *Therefore I say unto you, Take no thought for your life, what ye shall eat, or what ye shall drink; nor yet for your body, what ye shall put on. Is not the life more than meat, and the body than raiment.* But we are admonished to – Romans 8:37: *Nay, in all these things we are more*

CHAPTER EIGHT

than conquerors through him that loved us.

All you need is to be on the side of the Lord and let heaven's gate open for you and you will see that no other gate will close against your pursuit in life.

CHAPTER NINE

RELIGION IS SIN AGAINST DESTINY

What is religion? The Oxford Dictionary of English defines religion as follows:

- *the belief in and worship of a superhuman controlling power, especially a personal God or gods* – First, God is not superhuman. Secondly, God is not personal, He is a universal God. There is only one God; beside Him there is no other. This shows that what we should live for is the 'will' of God and not religion, if we must fulfil our destiny on Earth.

- *a particular system of faith and worship* – The worship of God is not a particular system, as there is no other system apart from the one set in place from creation. Our worship of God is a lifestyle of heaven.

CHAPTER NINE

- *a pursuit or interest followed with great devotion* – we don't have a special interest. We are only doing the will of God – nothing personal is attached.

If we look at the above reasoning, we will discover that many are yet to know the Lord. My relationship with God is that he is a guide who directs my path, and I see myself as His instrument to be used wherever He needs my service. Those who don't put themselves to the use of the Lord are religious people, seeing their relationship with God as a means to an end, and as such all their prayers are filled with the need to know what to eat and drink and what clothing to wear.

Jesus didn't come to establish a religion, as many have believed. He came to set the Kingdom of God in place. A clear fact that He didn't introduce a religion is seen in His debunking of the religious practices of the Jews and the Samaritans in John 4:21-24: *Jesus saith unto her, Woman, believe me, the hour cometh, when ye shall neither in this mountain, nor yet at Jerusalem, worship the Father. Ye worship ye know not what:we know what we worship:for salvation is of the Jews. But the hour cometh, and now is, when the true worshippers shall worship the Father in spirit and in truth:for the Father*

CHAPTER NINE

seeketh such to worship him. God is a Spirit:and they that worship him must worship him in spirit and in truth.

Severally in the scriptures we see Jesus letting us know that what He came for was a gathering of a people who truly want to return to their creator. How can this be a religious practice? The parable of the sower explained to us that it wasn't a forceful act to get people into the Kingdom (Matthew 13:3-9). It has to do with willingness. We have seen all over the world how religion has been used to foment war and discord among the people. It is only in our Christian belief that people are not forced to come to God. This explains the fact that Christianity is living in accordance with the precepts of God. Religionists live to condemn others, and are careless about the restoration of human dignity in God, which is what we all need to become who God had created us to be – His image and likeness.

The following verses will explain the difference between religious practice and the expectation of the will of God, which we must execute if we must fulfil of destiny in the Lord:

- Religious practice believes – Matthew 5:43: *Thou shalt love thy neighbour, and hate thine enemy.* The will of God says – Matthew 5:44: *But I say unto you, Love your enemies, bless them that curse you, do good to them that hate you, and pray for them which despitefully use you, and persecute you.*

- Religious practices believe that the sun should only rise and shine on the righteous only, but the will of God thinks otherwise – Matthew 5:45: *That ye may be the children of your Father which is in heaven: for he maketh his sun to rise on the evil and on the good, and sendeth rain on the just and on the unjust.*

- Religious practice believes that we love and greet only those that love and greets us, but the will of God preaches otherwise – Matthew 5:46: *For if ye love them which love you, what reward have ye? do not even the publicans the same? And if ye salute your brethren only, what do ye more than others? do not even the publicans so.*

- Religious practice does not believe that humans need to be as perfect as God, but the will of God wishes that all men shall become as perfect as God, as it was in the beginning when Adam named the animals and all we see, and God accepted his judgement as final – Matthew 5:48: *Be ye therefore perfect, even as your Father which is in heaven is perfect.*

CHAPTER NINE

- Religious practice dwells in carnality, as we may see in the message of Paul to the people of Corinth who were already practising the Hellenic religion – 1 Corinthians 3:1-3: *And I, brethren, could not speak unto you as unto spiritual, but as unto carnal, even as unto babes in Christ. I have fed you with milk, and not with meat: for hitherto ye were not able to bear it, neither yet now are ye able. For ye are yet carnal: for whereas there is among you envying, and strife, and divisions, are ye not carnal, and walk as men.* Religious people don't desire strong spiritual knowledge. All they desire is feasting, wealth seeking, power struggle, etc., with the aim of mocking others who don't belong to them and accepting their practices, who they always wish to keep under their control. If ever they seek spiritual knowledge, it is for the oppression of people – carting away their hard-earned monies, with the promise of helping them out of their predicaments. In such a gathering, all you hear is offering and the continuous collection of levies. Those who intend to enslave others are already slaves of conscience.

- Religion encourages people to live in the flesh, acquiring material wealth and power to control others – Romans 8:7-8: *Because the carnal mind is enmity against God: for it is not subject to the law of God, neither indeed can be. So then they that are in the flesh cannot please God.* The will of God is that we store our treasure in heaven and live a life of the spirit so that we can attain the spiritual consciousness of God as we receive from the Holy Spirit daily to better our lives here on Earth - Romans 8:9: *But ye are not in the flesh, but in the Spirit, if so be that the Spirit of God dwell in you.*

Religious practices believe that by pushing the weight of oppression on others, we would attain high spiritual achievements and success in life. Religion kills the human conscience. Jesus Christ referred to this generation in Mathew 12:39 as an adulterous generation who seek after a sign: *But He answered and said to them, "An evil and adulterous generation seeks after a sign, and no sign will be given to it except the sign of the prophet Jonah.*

People only attend churches where the order of the day is miracles. Fake pastors, preachers and prophets have capitalised on this and are now devising means of extorting money from their congregations through faked miracles. There seems to be more evil now that we have so many churches than before. The truth is that in many of these new churches, the intent is to make money and leave the congregation hungry – without being fed with spiritual milk. Some churches have become bookstores where various books by their pastors are sold at too high a price, given the benefit of the information contained in the book to the congregation. Many have even turned their congregations' mind-sets from the Bible so that they are taught vaguely from their pastor's books instead. The word of God is scarce, even with the multitude of preachers all over the world.

The crazy love of money! The love of money has driven many people, including pastors, into all kinds of businesses. In the church, the old trading in the temple Jesus condemned is still in existence today. In 1 Timothy 6:9-10 this is well explained when the Bible said: *But those who desire to be rich fall into temptation and a snare, and into many foolish and harmful lusts which drown men in destruction and perdition. For the love of money is a root of all kinds of evil, for which some have strayed from the faith in their greediness, and pierced themselves through with many sorrows.*

It is evident that the reason for all human sorrows is rooted in our love for money. Sorrow is the offshoot of greed. The translation above referred to the effect of this greed as "piercing themselves". The piercing sensation of a needle is the reason why many people run from being injected in the hospital when they are sick. If we run from piercing objects, why then have we yielded to the temptation of running after money? In our society today I have grown to find out that the more you chase money the more sorrowful and unsettled you become. According to King Solomon, this is an evil affliction: *A man to whom God has given riches and wealth and honour, so that he lacks nothing for himself of all he desires; yet God does not give him power to eat of it, but a foreigner consumes it. This is vanity, and it is an evil affliction* - Ecclesiastes 6:2.

A stony and unrepentant heart! This seems to be a punishment to people God wants to use as guinea pigs to showcase his anger. The heart of stone first appeared in the Book of Exodus 4:21, when God told Moses that He would harden Pharaoh's heart: *And the LORD said to Moses, "When you go back to Egypt, see that you do all those wonders before Pharaoh which I have put in your hand. But I will harden his heart, so that he will not let the people go.*

It is painful to know that even with all the warnings in the Bible against evil, people still engage in it, despising God straight to His face. People have turned the word

"Grace" to mean the reason why they must still live in sin. Surely this world is doomed because the atrocities committed daily are more grievous than what the people of Sodom and Gomorrah did. We have priests committing homosexuality right in the church. Pastors who commit fornication or adultery or both only need to relocate to another town or another section of the same town to establish another ministry and you will see the crowd flooding their ministry. God told me in 2006 that many are lost even while they are in the church. Wicked pastors and preachers are deceived by them daily.

God is angry! The Bible says - Psalms 53:1-3: *The fool hath said in his heart, There is no God. Corrupt are they, and have done abominable iniquity: there is none that doeth good. God looked down from heaven upon the children of men, to see if there were any that did understand, that did seek God. Every one of them is gone back: they are altogether become filthy; there is none that doeth good, no, not one.*

The gravity of sin that envelops our world today is difficult to imagine. People are no longer scared of sin; it is a way of life – lies everywhere, many hearts are corrupt right from the womb and they are only waiting to unleash this sinful act on any prey that comes their way. Our thoughts are evil, we find flavour in offending God – it doesn't matter after - all there is still time to repent! Who said that? The days are evil and judgement draws near. Everyone needs to be aware that the kingdom of God is at hand and therefore repentance is a must if we are not going to lose our generation to the devil. In Psalm 53:4 David was angered by the fact that those who commit evil seem not to have knowledge of what they do when he asked: *Have the workers of iniquity no knowledge?* Christ concluded it this way in Luke 23:34: *Then said Jesus, Father, forgive them; for they know not what they do.*

Forgiveness is tied to your repentance – when you swim inside the ocean of sin, be sure of God's condemnation unless you repent.

All have sinned! Many keep hiding under sin by claiming that the Ten Commandments are dead and buried. God's patience should not be mistaken for foolishness. Christ sealed these commandments in what He called the greatest commandment. If you love God with all your life and also love your neighbour there is no way you can go against the Ten Commandments – Matthew 5:17-19.

CHAPTER NINE

There is a popular song titled *"This is my desire"* and the lyrics read thus;

This is my desire, to honour You
Lord with all my heart I worship You
all I have within me
I give You praise
all that I adore is in You

Chorus:
Lord I give You my heart
I give You my soul
I live for You alone
Every breath that I take
Every moment I'm awake
Lord have Your way in me.

Many of us have committed even more sins through the songs we sing. If you look closely at the lyrics, if you are a sinner you cannot sing that song because you are lying before God. How can you say you live for God alone when you are not ready to be a part of the great commission? Well the lyrics of the songs we sing are also testimonies against us – that we know what to do but we choose to do evil and forget about God. All the songs and hymns we sing will testify against us – how we have promised God in our song lyrics over and over again without repenting.

We have sinned greatly against God – right from the pulpit, the congregation and the world at large. How many of us obey God and carry out His will? How many of us do the will of the Father the way Jesus taught us? What is the seed of righteousness that was sown in our hearts as a result of the death of Christ? If we do not have a change of heart, we are surely going to sleep with Mr Roaring Lion-Satan in his blazing hellfire.

CHAPTER TEN

KEYS TO LIVING A FULFILLING DESTINY

Fulfilling our destiny give us an opportunity to excel in our chosen career, an opportunity to be remembered and an opportunity to bring out our own ideas. In order to live a life-fulfilling destiny, one needs the power to put things under control. To put things under control was referred to in the Bible as *'bound or loosed.'* Jesus wasn't trying to make a joke with Peter when he said he would need the keys of heaven to be able to succeed in his calling – Matthew 16:19: *And I will give unto thee the keys of the kingdom of heaven: and whatsoever thou shalt bind on earth shall be bound in heaven: and whatsoever thou shalt loose on earth shall be loosed in heaven.*

In Luke 11:52, one of the keys was revealed - *Woe*

CHAPTER TEN

unto you, lawyers! for ye have taken away the key of knowledge: ye entered not in yourselves, and them that were entering in ye hindered. The key of knowledge is what establishes people so that they do not run to and fro (Daniel 12:4). Closely related to knowledge are the keys of understanding and wisdom – Exodus 31:3: *And I have filled him with the spirit of God, in wisdom, and in understanding, and in knowledge, and in all manner of workmanship, To devise cunning works, to work in gold, and in silver, and in brass, And in cutting of stones, to set them, and in carving of timber, to work in all manner of workmanship.* Life involves putting intricate pieces together. The things we do daily are more like the works of a craftsman. And from what we just read in Exodus 31, we need specific and guided knowledge, wisdom and understanding in every facet of our lives to succeed.

Knowledge is useless until it is understood and put to work. It is the application that we call wisdom. Then we may reap the fruit – Proverbs 3:16: *Length of days is in her right hand; and in her left hand riches and honour.* Length of days, riches and honour, are what beautify our destinies, and make us joyful.

We now have three keys. We will now search for the

CHAPTER TEN

other keys and then go deeper into each of them, bringing out the juicy flavour that will enable us fulfil our destiny before the Lord.

An important key that the Lord opened up to us is found in John 4:23: *But the hour cometh, and now is, when the true worshippers shall worship the Father in spirit and in truth: for the Father seeketh such to worship him.* This is the key of perfect worship. When we do this our hearts yearns for His instructions and the Lord helps us with guiding instructions as we live daily. Psalm 27:4-6: *One thing have I desired of the Lord, that will I seek after; that I may dwell in the house of the Lord all the days of my life, to behold the beauty of the Lord, and to enquire in his temple. For in the time of trouble he shall hide me in his pavilion: in the secret of his tabernacle shall he hide me; he shall set me up upon a rock. And now shall mine head be lifted up above mine enemies round about me: therefore will I offer in his tabernacle sacrifices of joy; I will sing, yea, I will sing praises unto the Lord.* To worship 'in truth and in spirit' is to seek after the Lord, dwell in His house as royal priests, and look unto Him as the author and finisher of our faith. In the time of confusion, as you encounter challenges daily, He will be there to

CHAPTER TEN

hide you in His pavilion – where secrets will be released unto you so that your head will be lifted up again to continue the race of life before those who wished you wouldn't rise again.

You may also want to see the words of Psalms 15, for the qualities of those who make life work in their favour. The last verse of Psalms 15 says ... *he that doeth these things shall never be moved.* Here, David stated why the lines where falling for him in pleasant places in Psalms 16:6: *The lines are fallen unto me in pleasant places; yea, I have a goodly heritage*

The next key we will talk about is 'Power.' The importance of this key to our success is seen in Jesus' statement in Matthew 28:18: *And Jesus came and spake unto them, saying, All power is given unto me in heaven and in earth.* With this power in place, creation became possible - John 1:3: *All things were made by him; and without him was not any thing made that was made.* This was why Paul explained that the reason he was able to carry on with his destiny was that he was receiving strength from Christ - Philippians 4:13: *I can do all things through Christ which strengtheneth me.* So the next time you are on your knees to pray, ask the Lord for His

CHAPTER TEN

power. Without it, you become fed up with life so quickly. The zeal and courage to continue to face the challenges of life is hinged on this spiritual empowerment to make things happen in your favour.

So far we have been able to bring out five keys which I feel can set anyone on the pedestal of success – Knowledge, Understanding, Wisdom, Worship, and Power. I will use the five fingers of the left hand to explain what each stands for – thumb (Knowledge), index finger (Understanding), middle finger (Wisdom), ring finger (Worship), and little finger (Power). The ring finger is where we usually place our wedding ring, signifying identity, dedication, and faithfulness to our vows of submission – the covenant in place. There is no other key that would take this place than worship. Now, worship goes with praise and prayer. In submissive worship, our prayers filter into the nostrils of God as sweet-smelling incense. And the more this happens, the more we put Him in remembrance of the terms of our covenant with Him.

Why am I using the left hand fingers for this analogy, to enable us understand the keys to living a fulfilling destiny? Let see Job 23:9: *On the left hand when he is working...* (ESV) – the left hand contains secrets that put things to work. We also have this from Songs 2:6: *His left hand is under my head...* - the left hand is more conveniently placed under the head to rest on. Ezekiel 39:3: *And I will smite thy bow out of thy left hand* - the bow is kept on the left hand. Again, the left hand was used as a reservoir for oil of sprinkling in the Old Testament – Leviticus 14:26: *And the priest shall pour of the oil into the palm of his own left hand.* Now that we have this understanding, I encourage you to see beyond the physical so that we can be on the same spiritual page. The keys we explained above are reservoirs to the secrets of greatness. Once we can apply these and let them become a part of our lives, there is no way we won't succeed.

How do we now employ these keys? This is the subject of the next chapter.

CHAPTER ELEVEN

NINETY PER CENT SPIRITUAL, TEN PER CENT SOCIAL

Try and plan your life weekly in such a way that you spend 90% of your free hours on growing your spiritual life, such as writing Christian books, praying, praising, recording songs in the studio, meditating, and any other spiritual promptings that the Holy Spirit would relate to you from your Lord. You can spend the remaining 10% on anything social – making phone calls to greet people aside from praying and encouraging them, outing with your family when it is needed, etc. The basis for this is to ensure one is connected to the spiritual throughout the day. You may figure out a different ratio for yourself, but try to keep it a routine activity.

CHAPTER ELEVEN

What keeps the iceberg floating is the 90% of its volume which is under water. King David says in Psalms 42:7: *...all thy waves and thy billows are gone over me.* This means that he was totally submerged in the spiritual. Jesus says that we need to drink His water – John 7:38: *He that believeth on me, as the scripture hath said, out of his belly shall flow rivers of living water.* There will only be a flow of water out of our belly when we are soaked in the water and have drunk enough.

Ninety per cent spiritual presence also implies that you are spiritually alert at all times, because the days are evil, and the devil is moving about like a roaring lion, looking for destinies to murder. Our 90% spiritual presence will surely keep us on our feet, to know when the enemy is invading our territorial boundaries. We should be watchful for seductive scenes, possible acts of cheating, an environment prepared for lies to take root, etc. - we are told that God is a watchman who never sleeps nor slumber – Psalms 121:4. If God is spiritually there He is one hundred per cent there because He is a spirit, and we are encouraged to be as perfect as God – Matthew 5:48, ninety per cent spiritual alertness demand on us shouldn't be too much to ask for.

CHAPTER ELEVEN

Now, how do I keep my spiritual alertness? I do it through meditation. I pick up a verse of the Bible, and meditate on it continually. I also send several questions into the spiritual realm – why is this like this? Why is this brother suffering? Why are the seasons no longer as they were? What will happen to this company in five years' time? What will happen to the world with the way sin is increasing? All these are spiritually focused questions. Sometimes you will become absent-minded. Sometime, it will seem as if one is talking to oneself, which is termed soliloquizing.

Another thing I want us to note is that there is also a possibility that ninety per cent of some of the problems we are able to surmount physically are controlled in the spiritual. I recounted a story my parents told me at the beginning. If it had not been for the anointing of the Lord that is upon me from the womb, my mother would have had a miscarriage, had my dad shot that antelope used as a manipulating object. So we would see that once we address our security with the anointing, our destiny will not suffer from the fangs of miscarriage. This implies that there is a place for spiritual deliverance – ancestral altars and vows made by our forefathers, though I don't give

CHAPTER ELEVEN

so much attention to these, because the love of God has delivered me from this, and the faith I have in the Lord is bulletproof enough to neutralise any satanic caricature planted in my vicinity. I am not so happy when I see people being over frightened by the manoeuvrings of the devil. These people haven't learnt the ways of God yet.

To me, Saturdays are spiritual purification and sanctification days. I see the act of sanitary observation as both keeping the physical surroundings from infection as well as the spiritual surroundings free from satanic intrusions. Keep it 90% spiritual – 10% social. Be alert – the devil is cunning! Mind what you hear, see and smell. Be in charge of your physical senses, and your spiritual awareness will improve. Sense it – act accordingly.

CHAPTER TWELVE

HOW YOU HAVE FARED

Now, it is time for you to recall to memory how you have fared so far on Earth. You are going to write in plain language, and in a simple sentence:

- What is your vision?
- What is the vision of your parents?
- What is the vision of your village/town/country?
- What is the vision of your church?

Now that you are done with this, you would now answer the following questions, with compelling evidence that anyone who know you can attest to be true any time anyday:

- What is your contribution to other people's success?
- What is your contribution to your own success?

CHAPTER TWELVE

- What is your contribution to society?
- What is your contribution to the success of the vision of your church?

If we say that each of these carry twenty-five per cent, can you fix a number in front of each, and see how they total up? Seventy-five per cent is good enough, below fifty per cent is not ideal. This will definitely take you some time to complete. Please be very sincere with the information you are putting down, because this will help you a great deal as you go through this mystery of life called 'destiny.' Your vision can never be in isolation, there is always a part that will interlock with another's vision.

One common thing with destiny is seen below:

- People were given a destiny to fulfil.
- They ran with it.
- Others assisted them.
- And they all succeeded together.

This shows that we achieve our own destiny in each other's destiny. This is why the saying goes that 'a single tree cannot make a forest.'

To be able to be help in supporting others' vision and

thereby fulfil your own destiny, one needs to see spiritually. Spiritual focus has to do with what the human senses perceive, because these are what manipulate your thoughts. This is why our senses have to be tuned spiritually. Hence, Christ told them that those who have ears should listen. Physical seeing is possible when there is a physical source of light, such as the moon, the sun, an electric bulb, fire etc. In the same way, spiritual seeing is possible when there is a spiritual illumination source – Isaiah 42:16. Jesus is that source of light to spiritual vision.

Spiritual seeing – Joel 2:28, 2 Chronicles 26:5

- Spiritual seeing is the secret behind focus.
- Spiritual eyes make you see beyond your present situation.
- It is the secret power behind success.
- When you see your afflictions in the physical, you fight them in the spiritual.

Physical seeing

- For physical direction – Psalm 32:8
- Brings distraction – 1 John 2:16
- Brings fear – 2 Timothy 1:7

CHAPTER TWELVE

- Brings pride – Proverbs 16:18
- Brings envy - Numbers 5:14
- Brings lust - 2 Peter 2:14, 1 Kings 22:21
- Powers your desires - Genesis 13:14

The saying goes, 'Pride goes before a fall' – Proverbs 16:18. This is the result of seeing with the physical eyes. Your spiritual eyes control your mortal being and your physical body, and they have to be well tuned through the anointing – Revelation 3:18: *and anoint thine eyes with eyesalve, that thou mayest see.* Once this is done, they can be of great help to our wellbeing here on Earth, and our mistakes would be greatly reduced. What bring pain to us are the mistakes we make daily.

Another thing we need to know is that life starts from hope. Being hopeful is what builds your faith in Christ. This faith in Jesus is what leads to the love we have for God and our neighbour. To have faith, you need a lot of encouragement, and to be encouraged you must first be hopeful. Love is the ability to please the people around you. Love soothes your pains, it makes you want to live, and it makes you want to understand why certain things happen to you. Our faith cannot yield its fruit without love. This is why we must love our neighbours.

CHAPTER TWELVE

Humility gives birth to joy. Not until you are humble may you have joy, because it is only then you know that you need the knowledge to help you succeed. That is when you will not mind your age but stoop low to learn from others. You can then be patient, even to seek more avenues of success, because there is joy in your heart. And finally you must be ready to be accountable for all you do. Prudence is keenly related to accountability. Many people, especially women, don't want their partners to ask them how they spent their money. We must be ready to account for everything we do in the physical.

If you would need people to join you in driving the vision you have, you must also be able to persuade them to follow you. What then is the act of persuasion?

Women are very good at persuasion. Those who are close to their mothers will certainly know how to persuade people to get something from them. But often people persuade others by creating seductive scenes. This is sin against your destiny.

We may now define the Act of Persuasion. Persuasion is at work to:

- Influence
- Advise

CHAPTER TWELVE

- Urge
- Give an opinion
- Argue your points
- Affiliate with other establishments to seek assistance.

I see 'The Act of Persuasion' therefore as *the action of an individual envisioned to yield an intended result through arguing, influencing, convincing, urging, affiliating etc., with the persons, people or a defined group of persons who have a predefined way of life or belief.*

We will now discuss what makes up the act of persuasion. How do we persuade others? We can get a clue from Mark 1:17: *And Jesus said to them, Follow Me, and I will make you become fishers of men.*

From here we can see that the 'act of persuasion' is made up of two parts: the 'request statement', *follow me*, and the 'persuasive element', *fishers of men*. They were already fishermen, so the language wasn't vague to them. Their thoughts were varied on hearing what Jesus said. They would get the implication of Jesus' invitation through the act of trying to understand what He said. They may have thought, Jesus was going to train them and they would learn how to recruit more men who would assist them in the sea to get more fish. We would see that the 'persuasive element' here was striking and straight to the point. We would now see how this works out so that you are empowered to start persuading people to follow your dreams and aspirations in life.

- The Request Statement: The quality of the 'request statement' has a lot to do, because this is the first point of attraction. Its main role is to negotiate the agreement path. If the request is offensive you may find it difficult to get the target audience to listen to you. The request statement can be verbal or non-verbal: verbal request statements are voice activated. A woman's voice attracts more attention than a male voice. Also the cry of a baby attracts. This is why a woman preacher may get more people to show interest in repenting than a male preacher, because of the use of emotionally persuasive words. Non-verbal includes the display of good character, neat and beautiful dressing habit, cultured manners, etc.

- The Persuasive Element: When we visit places, the environment may be the main reason why we would want to go back there again. A man in love would look for a persuasive element, say a bunch of flowers, to win his heartthrob.

CHAPTER TWELVE

Many of us don't get answers to our prayers because we lack persuasive power. God informs us to testify against Him, in Micah 6:3. Abraham took a step of faith when he washed the legs of the Angels – Genesis 18:3 – 10: *... My Lord, if now I have found favour in thy sight, pass not away, I pray thee, from thy servant. Let a little water, I pray you, be fetched, and wash your feet, and rest yourselves under the tree. ... And Abraham ran unto the herd, and fetcht a calf tender and good, and gave it unto a young man; and he hasted to dress it ... And they said unto him, Where is Sarah thy wife? And he said, Behold, in the tent. And he said, I will certainly return unto thee according to the time of life; and, lo, Sarah thy wife shall have a son.* We can see persuasion at work. Abraham persuaded the Lord with wholehearted loyalty and humility, and he was rewarded. The woman with the alabaster oil received forgiveness because she displayed an act that was so convincing before the Lord – Luke 7:37,38,47: *Wherefore I say unto thee, Her sins, which are many, are forgiven; for she loved much: but to whom little is forgiven, the same loveth little. ...Her sins, which are many, are forgiven; for she loved much ...*

People talk to those who always listen to them.

Encouraging people requires a lot of persuasive power, and they want you to listen to them. Abraham could speak to the Angels because they listened.

Why should we be involved in persuasion?

- To win souls – Acts 26:28, 2 Corinthians. 5:11, Galatians 1:10.
- To seek help to build the church – Leviticus 1:2.
- To seek help for ourselves.
- To encourage people.
- To intercede/plead on behalf of others.

How should we persuade people?

- Through the use of words we communicate our hearts.
- The way we act displays sincerity.
- The way we laugh and smile also encourages people to listen to us.
- The way we help people out of a situation, as in the story of the good Samaritan.
- By advising them positively, they will succeed and begin to add value to society.

- By providing for their needs when we have, they would join us in the vision we bear.
- Through the word of our testimonies, they will learn to trust in tomorrow.
- Through the stories of people in the Bible, they will also pick moral lessons to beautify their lives.

Gains of Persuasion

- An effective tool in evangelism, as we encounter people daily and communicate with them using persuasive skills.
- An effective tool in prayer, as we will know how to put our words together and across to the Lord.
- An effective tool in seeking help from people, when we are in need of assistance.
- An effective tool for the demonstration of leadership excellence, as the leader relates with those he leads in a persuasive manner, rather than in an autocratic manner.
- An effective tool in business to win customers during product promotion through using advertising tools, such as employing persuasive elements in the advertisement.

CHAPTER TWELVE

Now that you have learned all these, you will turn over to the next page for a continuation of this discussion on understanding your destiny, and then after you have applied what you have learnt, and have begun adding value to your life and others, you will have to return to the beginning of this chapter and answer the questions again, to see how you have fared.

CHAPTER THIRTEEN

SEE YOUR DESTINY THROUGH THE EYES OF OTHERS

Now that you have seen how you have fared in the last chapter, let's now see how you can achieve even more. When we are employed in an establishment where we earn a living, there we can see our destiny being shaped by what God has used others to establish. Jesus says in John 4:37-38: *And herein is that saying true, One soweth, and another reapeth. I sent you to reap that whereon ye bestowed no labour: other men laboured, and ye are entered into their labours.* Except the Lord instructs otherwise, there is no need to reinvent the wheel. Key into other people's destiny – this is why someone had to

CHAPTER THIRTEEN

be there before you were born. Jesus didn't need to prepare the way because John the Baptist had already done that. He didn't need also to give them the law but to rather fulfil, because Moses had given the law. Our destiny is in the vision of others in most cases.

A wife cannot start reinventing her own vision when one has been given to the husband. If there is high disparity between their visions and hobbies, then the home is torn apart – they may not have been made for each other. My wife was in the choir and dedicated to the service of God in the Catholic Church to the extent that the reverend father knew her by name, and she later became the school chapel prefect. Her marrying one who would now serve in the Altar of the Lord was therefore already ordained. This shows that she had been prepared for the task ahead – her destiny.

Abraham saw ahead of his days. He obeyed and followed God to ensure he fulfilled the will of God in his life. Many of us are living today through the vision of others. The company we work in was the idea of someone else. The dress you are putting on right now is someone else's design. Even the food you are eating was someone else's idea. Here we will be seeing what others

CHAPTER THIRTEEN

did, as the Lord laid it in their hearts, and how these acts have added value to the life we live today.

Often people really don't want to serve, but there lies the secret of success. In the Bible we see that Lot, Abraham's nephew, had left him before God gave Abraham the vision of his inheritance (Genesis 13:14-17). This is the problem many people usually have with a visionary because they are so impatient to see the vision to the end with the visionary. Often when a servant of God asks to see those who started with him, only a handful will raise their hands. And many of those who had left are still seen trying to figure out what life has in store for them. The servant of God receives vision; it is left for him to make it plain so that others can read it as they run - Habakkuk 2:2; they run because things aren't ok. If as they run they would be able to discern the vision, they would be delivered. When I see this, what comes to my mind is the word of Jesus – Luke 21:19: *In your patience possess ye your souls.*

I will also advise you to seek the service of a servant of God so that you can partake in the anointing upon him. I have heard complaints that many people do call the 'God of the servant of God' instead of the God of Abraham, Isaac, and Jacob, when they pray. They

CHAPTER THIRTEEN

honestly forgot that Elisha called on the God of Elijah – 2 Kings 2:14: *And he took the mantle of Elijah that fell from him, and smote the waters, and said, Where is the Lord **God of Elijah**? and when he also had smitten the waters, they parted hither and thither: and Elisha went over.* And that Nebuchadnezzar referred to the God of Daniel: *The king answered unto Daniel, and said, Of a truth it is, that **your God** is a God of gods, and a Lord of kings, and a revealer of secrets, seeing thou couldest reveal this secret* - Daniel 2:47. Such people only display arrogance and envy. If you want to partake in his anointing, start by reading his books. Elisha didn't know any other power but the one upon Elijah. The Jewish people only read the books of Moses and those of the prophets. If you will read the book of Saint Paul, why not read that of your pastor? If you hate your pastor, how do you expect him to minister grace to you? The Lord has given Him to you to be a help when the need arises - 2 Chronicle 26:5: *He sought God in the days of Zechariah, who had understanding in the visions of God; and as long as he sought the Lord, God made him prosper.*

When you involve God in your vision, you will surely succeed. The servant of God will guide you with scripture evidence for what is right and what is not right for you

CHAPTER THIRTEEN

to do. The message you hear on Sunday is general, but when you engage him, you will receive specific visions related to what you are about embarking on. People have sometimes ask me why I am insensitive to social issues, and I have always replied that the Lord employed me to address spiritual issues, and so my attention is 90% spiritual, 10% social.

The character of the 12 Disciples is a compelling one. Did the Disciples see their destiny through the eyes of Jesus? To some extent, they did not at the beginning – Mark 10:28: *Then Peter began to say unto him, Lo, we have left all, and have followed thee.* And we would also see Peter being used three times by the devil against the will of God after Jesus had pronounced Him the leader whom He would hand over to, in Matthew 16:17 – first in Matthew 16:23, where Jesus rebuked him knowing that the devil had possessed him to challenge Jesus' destiny, secondly, in Mark 14:72, Peter denied Jesus three times, and thirdly, in John 21, Peter took the disciples into the sea, abandoning the vision set for them by Jesus. The Lord came to the final rescue, and with the Holy Spirit empowerment (Acts 2), each of them fulfilled their destiny in Jesus' vision.

CHAPTER THIRTEEN

I have learnt that when people set their own fires, the heat generated is often not as much as when people gather firewood together and set it all on fire. The warmth from such a fire will be far-reaching. I would encourage us to gather together rather than gather separately. We should learn to submit to leadership authorities. We should not allow the quest for money to ruin our great destiny. Someone must be the leader, while others follow.

CHAPTER FOURTEEN

BE BOLD AND CONFRONT YOUR FEARS

Many people are where they are today, not making headway in their pursuit of destiny, because they haven't been able to confront their fears. To confront one's fears, one needs the spirit of boldness. Many people see boldness as a show of arrogant behaviour, but that is not the case. The demonstration of boldness has a lot to do with confidence.

- Boldness is what makes you confront your past. It is what makes you know you need to change the way you are living. Boldness is what makes you repent from your sins. Foolishness deprives you of your

CHAPTER FOURTEEN

success, but boldness strengthens your spirit. Boldness is the spirit of every successful individual.

- Why do you need boldness? It is the achiever's spirit. It is a push from the inside. The vigour to achieve is the root of boldness. The strength to go against all odds and still succeed is the whole essence of being bold. It is the opposite of feeblemindedness.

- Boldness is fearless. No believer is fearful. If you are the fearful type, then you are not a believer. God has not given you the spirit of fear, so why the fear (2 Timothy 1:7)? You are a lion in Christ, with all the powers in the world in your hands because the keys of heaven are with you. Jesus has given us the power to tread on serpents and scorpions, and over all the power of the enemy, and nothing shall by any means hurt us (Luke 10:19). A thousand will fall by your left hand side, and ten thousand by your right hand side, but it shall never come near us because every demonic and satanic obstacle against our success has been destabilised (Psalms 91:7). That is what God said in Isaiah 42:16. The word of God says in, Deuteronomy 28:7: *they shall come out against thee one way, and flee before thee seven ways,* in other words their plans have been shattered.

CHAPTER FOURTEEN

- Boldness is action. Some people are bold, but they don't take action to put that boldness into useful work - rather they see boldness as innate rudeness in insulting elders and those in leadership. Arrogance, disrespect, attitudinal foolishness, bullying, bossiness, folly and anything that will lead you into sin are not boldness.

- Boldness is making the right decision. I have also seen people who see themselves as being bold but lack the willpower to take the right decisions. They are seldom pushed back by the challenges they foresee. Bold people are those who tell you to cross the bridge when you get there. Bold people are what the world is lacking, and all the believers who know for sure that the spirit they receive from God can do all things are wallowing in self-condemnation of the sins they committed yesterday which Satan is using to keep them under his feet, instead of them always being above, as declared by God in Deuteronomy 28:13.

- Boldness is correction. Bold people do the right thing for others to see, appreciate and imitate to better the world. Not until your actions bring correction are you bold. Bold people go against the crowd to win. They are driven by results and not by perceptions. We have people who will blacklist others to make themselves shine, but that shine is only for a while because the sun of truth will soon shine stronger and their woes will be spread in the open for all to see. People don't shine through gossip; we shine through making amends, and making corrections where others have gone wrong and being a source of joy to all and sundry.

- Boldness doesn't procrastinate. Many believers procrastinate a lot. While unbelievers are busy capturing the world, these sets of believers claim this world is not their own and therefore they are just passing through. Well I don't know where they got that doctrine. Christ said we should pray for the kingdom of God to be established on Earth. God spoke of a new Heaven and a new Earth. Action-oriented fellows are success-oriented too. And they are those who don't procrastinate. This is the same set of people God is looking for to win souls for Him. If you are the procrastinating type, pray that God will take away the spirit of procrastination from you.

- Boldness is excellency of knowledge in action. It is that action that brings deadness to life - Ecclesiastes

CHAPTER FOURTEEN

7:12: *For wisdom is a defence, and money is a defence: but the excellency of knowledge is, that wisdom giveth life to them that have it.*

This spirit can be seen in the following heralds of boldness in the Bible.

The boldness of Miriam, the elder sister of Moses, was on display when she watched over her brother Moses. Today Moses is a man through whom the law was given. The importance of Miriam in Moses' life cannot be overemphasized. Miriam was used by God to care for baby Moses, and she was endowed with wisdom, which was why she opted that the daughter of Pharaoh should give the baby to someone who later became Moses' mother to care for him. Some people would have run out at the sight of the princess because of fear. Boldness enables you to approach the high and low in society and get results.

Rehab also displayed boldness despite being a prostitute who should have felt unqualified to be in the midst of God's ordained people. The citizens of Jericho came looking for the spice, but Rehab hid them and protected them from assault. Then she demanded a

CHAPTER FOURTEEN

favour from them because 'one good turn deserves another.' Many wives think they can get anything from their husband with force. The Bible taught us that when men ask for something from God, they always use the words "if I have found favour in your sight". We should be ready to ask for favour when we know we have satisfied our conscience that we have done well. The Bible also taught us that a man's gift makes a way for him (Proverbs 18:16). You can never be bold when you have no testimony. What have you done that is so spectacular for the favour you seek? God had asked the Israelites to testify against Him in Micah 6:3. If you know you merit that favour, go ahead and ask with boldness and you shall be rewarded.

The Bible also tells us to know that Daniel was ten times better in wisdom (Daniel 1:20). This is the quality that announced him in Babylon. He was a stranger and a slave, but he outshone his colleagues because he had a peculiar spirit, the spirit of boldness. It was the boldness in him that made him tell the king's butler that he should be examined after ten days to see if there was a need for him to eat from the king's delicacies. It was wisdom that brought and established him as a man of regard and honour in the king's palace.

CHAPTER FOURTEEN

The Shunammite woman invited Elisha, the Man of God, into her home. She received a child out of this regard, and when the child was down with illness, she went to the source of her initial help. Her conscience was clear and so she was able to still maintain the relationship. Many people run out of God's house the moment they get what they are looking for, and when trouble comes, they won't be able to look into the eyes of the servant of God.

The widow Elisha ministered to was able to collect empty jars from people because she knew she had no enemy within who would deny her. If she had been the troublesome type, she would definitely not go out looking for empty jars because her surroundings are filled with those she always quarrels with. Her blessings would have been short-changed by the number of enemies she had.

Nehemiah overcame the threats of his mockers, who saw him as feeble-minded when he championed the supervision of the building of the fence around Jerusalem.

Zerubbabel revisited the status quo by building the house of the Lord. Many leaders are in the process of trying to start new projects without completing existing

CHAPTER FOURTEEN

ones because, as it were, they were started by an administration that is not theirs.

Esther decided that if she would perish, let it be, and she fearlessly petitioned the king to save her people. We see here that her destiny was at work. This was because her heart was clean too. Many wives cannot talk to their husbands because they are guilty of one sin or the other against them; it is the same with husbands who cannot face their wives.

Mary the Mother of Jesus told Him that their wine had finished and commanded the servants in the wedding feast to do whatever He said, despite Jesus telling her His time had not come. That is boldness and confidence. Many of us don't know what we have around us. Many mothers today don't know who their child is.

Rebeccah knew the children in her womb, Esau and Jacob, after she had communed with God (Genesis 25:22). Many mothers are in the habit of nagging and find it hard to appear before God. Their prayers lack the right substance to invoke God's blessings because they are being overrun by guilt.

From all these stories, we can start to understand what boldness is all about. Boldness is finding a genuine solution to move ahead, even when everyone thinks it cannot be done. It is the spirit that makes you believe in yourself. I have always been seen as not capable. People make judgments about me from a distance, saying I am not brave enough. They also saw Jesus as the son of a carpenter too (Mark 6:3), and Moses as a stammerer who was trying to force himself to be a prince and a judge over his people – Exodus 2:14. He finally achieved it of course!

My father looked at me one morning and said he regretted having me as his elder son, because he wasn't sure I would ever become somebody. Yea! When people despise you, and you are bold inside with the zeal to achieve, the sky is your limit, because God is the father to the fatherless and the hope to the hopeless. Come unto God today and His milk and meat will satisfy you.

A measure of boldness

From what we have discussed so far, we know now that the measure of boldness you display is related to the level of your faith and wisdom and the powers that work in you. We are made to realise that out of the abundance of the heart, we utter words with our mouth. Saint Paul says

CHAPTER FOURTEEN

(Romans 12:3): *For I say, through the grace given unto me, to every man that is among you, not to think of himself more highly than he ought to think; but to think soberly, according as God hath dealt to every man the measure of faith.*

To everyone, God has given a measure of faith, which is boldness in this instance; He has also given the 'will' to exercise it. In Acts 1:8, Christ told the disciples that they had to receive a measure of the spirit of boldness before they could exercise the faith they had received by believing in Him. You could also see that throughout the book of Acts and the Epistles that the disciples actually exercised this measure of boldness in their exploits.

To this end, I will quickly tell you that your exploits are directly proportional to the measure of faith in you. The same goes for boldness. Your achievement is a measure of your faith and your faith is displayed in your boldness. And in your boldness, the wisdom in you is made manifest. The measure of wisdom in you is what announces you, and everyone will know that God speaks through you. We are told that without faith, no one can please God (Hebrews 11:6). This is true because God wants your light to shine before men who will in turn give him praise for your sake – Matthew 5:16. But when you are not achieving physically and spiritually, then you are robbing God of His hard-earned Glory through the death of Jesus Christ.

From this we can say that:

- The measure of boldness in a believer is a function of the word of God in him/her and the wisdom in him/her. Jeremiah 8:9 concludes that unless you have the word of God in you, you will always be put to shame: *The wise men are ashamed, they are dismayed and taken: lo, they have rejected the word of the Lord; and what wisdom is in them?* No one who is in shame can be bold enough to confront his/her fears.

Now that we know that boldness is the opposite of shame, we will be using some mathematical relationship to drive home our discussion. Therefore:

$$\text{Boldness} = \text{Word of God} \times \text{Wisdom} \quad - (1a)$$

Hence,

$$\text{Boldness} = \text{Holy Spirit} \times \text{Wisdom} \quad - (1b)$$

The Holy Spirit is the wisdom of God in action. This wisdom of God can only have root in your life when the wisdom in you is not worldly. If you belong to

Satan then the Holy Spirit can never manifest in your life and you will become foolish instead of being bold. Joy is what gladdens the heart of God, and it is also what moves the Holy Spirit into action.

- Also in Genesis 26 we are told that Isaac heard the word of God; he had faith and sowed in the land and he became rich.

Thus,

Achievement = Word of God x Faith in God - (2a)

And since the word of God is the Holy Spirit of God, we have,

Achievement = Holy Spirit x Faith in God - (2b)

This is why in Matthew 5:16, Jesus said our achievement as believers should be spellbound in such a way that the world will know what stuff we are made of. They will know that the word of God dwells in you, which is the root of the faith you have in God. This is why in James 2:20 the Bible says - *But wilt thou know, O vain man, that faith without works is dead.* Our achievement is our works, and it is the demonstration of what manner of spirit lives in us.

From the discussion above, we can now equate the equations above:

CHAPTER FOURTEEN

Boldness = Holy Spirit x Wisdom - (1b)

Achievement = Holy Spirit x Faith - (2b)

Therefore from 2b,

Holy Spirit = Achievement ÷ Faith - (2c)

This is very important, in that it shows that the Holy Spirit is given to those who are ready for exploits in life. And from 2c, we would see that our sustenance of the Holy Spirit in our lives is related to our achievements and our faith in God. Meaning also that the reason many don't feel the Holy Spirit presence is because they don't have faith.

Now we will see how this works out. The values for each of the variables above will be as follows:

- If one has the wisdom of God, the value will be '1'

- If one has no wisdom of God, the value will be '0'

- If one has Holy Spirit, the value will be '1'

- If one does not have the Holy Spirit, the value will be '0'

- If one has Faith, the value is '1'

- If one does not have Faith, the value is '0'

CHAPTER FOURTEEN

Then we would see that, for:

Wisdom = 1, Holy Spirit = 1

Boldness = 1 x 1 = 1

This individual will be bold enough to confront his/her fears.

If also Faith = 1,

Achievement = 1 x 1 = 1

This individual will have evidence of achievements in life to show.

Now, let's look at a scenario that is prevalent in the world today; where people have worldly achievements but they don't have the Holy Spirit. To explain this, we will substitute 2c into 1b.

Thus, Boldness = Achievement x Wisdom ÷ Faith

This gives:

Boldness x Faith = Achievements x Wisdom - (3)

This assertion can be confirmed in the book of Daniel 1:17-20. In verse 17 we are told that God gave them knowledge, which means they have faith in God. In verse 19 the king communed with them and they spoke with boldness. This is a multiplying effect. They have faith, they believed in God and they went ahead to showcase what they had inside when the king confronted them. It is only bold people that can commune with kings and queens, because they are known to seek after wisdom, and they have wisdom to rule and judge. So talking to a king demands that you must be filled with wisdom and you require confidence to do that. Confidence is the product of faith and wisdom.

Further down in verse 20 the Bible tells us that they were ten times better (achievement) in wisdom and understanding than any other wise man in Babylon.

The level of faith and boldness you display also shows the level of confidence you can exercise. That is,

Confidence = Boldness x Faith - (4)

So that,

Confidence = Achievements x Wisdom - (5)

Implying that our confidence grows when we have the wisdom of God residing in us, and we can see what we have achieved with the wisdom as a testimony of the work of God in our lives. Those who have no wisdom of God, though they have

CHAPTER FOURTEEN

worldly achievements, have no confidence in themselves when confronted. And here the equation would be:

Confidence = Achievement x 0 = 0 'zero'

We also have those who cheated to pass interviews, and you would see them exhibiting zero confidence when confronted with issues of life.

If the wisdom in you is not founded on the word of God, then your Wisdom will not have a godly substance. The less your wisdom, the less your confidence to succeed and survive. In the same way, if you are failing in life, your confidence will also wither. You can correct this now by exercising the spirit of God in you. Study more of the word of God and you will see the spirit of boldness interacting with your faith to produce the much-needed confidence to achieve and the wisdom to excel more than ten times ahead of others.

It is the Holy Spirit of God that powers the wisdom in us. *Wisdom therefore defines your ability to rightly apply the word of God to issues that confront you.*

CHAPTER FOURTEEN

The works of boldness

We may now see some works of boldness in our lives:

- Secret to Signs and Wonders: The Lord promised us that those that believe in Him would experience a super flow of abundance, signs and wonders. The secret to experiencing Signs and Wonders is boldness. If you don't testify about the name of Jesus in the open with so much courage and boldness, Signs and Wonders will never manifest in your life. You will be struggling to survive. The Bible says in, Acts 14:3: *Long time therefore abode they speaking boldly in the Lord, which gave testimony unto the word of his grace, and granted Signs and Wonders to be done by their hands.*

- Brings recognition and help: The spirit of boldness opens up your understanding and you are able to speak out amidst mistakes. Moses stammered, but when he encountered God he became a respected leader. Jesus Christ was respected at the age of 12 when He taught at the temple. David was bold enough to face Goliath because he had the spirit of boldness in him. Many of us fail in business because we lack the spirit of boldness - the spirit to venture into new frontiers. Many are only interested in doing what others are doing. Some don't even display uniqueness, because the activating spirit of excellence is lacking in them. The spirit of excellence is driven by the spirit of boldness. Before Daniel excelled, he always displayed boldness. First in Daniel 1, we are told that he and his friends rejected the king's delicacy even to their own detriment. In chapter 2, he also told the king to wait, and later on he told the king his woeful end and what would happen to his kingdom (Daniel 4). Many of us are eye service workers and therefore do not see reasons for improvements. Here again, we would see boldness in display - Acts 18:26: *And he began to speak boldly in the synagogue: whom when Aquila and Priscilla had heard, they took him unto them, and expounded unto him the way of God more perfectly.*

- Refusal to disobey God: Many of us only tell the truth on Sundays in church when we read the Bible, because the words we read are truth. Apart from Sundays, we live in lies throughout the week and never take note of it as an attitude that is against the will of God. Hear now, what three young men who trusted in God said - Daniel 3:17-18 *If it be so, our God whom we serve is able to deliver us from the burning fiery furnace, and he will deliver us out of thine hand, O king. But if not, be it known unto thee, O king, that we will not serve thy gods, nor worship the golden image which thou hast set up.*

CHAPTER FOURTEEN

- Taking the right decision: Our trust in the Lord makes us exercise the boldness in us against all odds – taking the right decision even when it will take our lives - Nehemiah 6:11 *And I said, Should such a man as I flee?*

- Fearless defence of God's name: David stood firm to defend the name of the Lord. Many of us push His name under the table in order to receive favour from men – what a shame. 1 Samuel 17:45: *Then said David to the Philistine, Thou comest to me with a sword, and with a spear, and with a shield: but I come to thee in the name of the Lord of hosts, the God of the armies of Israel, whom thou hast defied.* Also we would see Elijah challenging the powers that be in his days, despite God preserving seven thousand who were to work for Him – 1 Kings 19:18. Hear what Elijah said - 1 Kings 18:15: *And Elijah said, As the Lord of hosts liveth, before whom I stand, I will surely shew myself unto him to day.*

- Execute the word of faith: Many of us cannot exercise faith that can move a mountain, because we lack the spirit of boldness. See this - Numbers 16:47-48 *And Aaron took as Moses commanded, and ran into the midst of the congregation; and, behold, the plague was begun among the people: and he put on*

CHAPTER FOURTEEN

incense, and made an atonement for the people. And he stood between the dead and the living; and the plague was stayed. The moment the word came, Aaron put it to work. Many of us doubt the released Rhema because we lack understanding.

- Ability to talk with God: If you are bold, it will show in your prayers because you are in charge of the praying session and God will know that you mean business. We would also want to see - Exodus 33:18: *And he said, I beseech thee, shew me thy glory.* And Genesis 18:22-32: *And the men turned their faces from thence, and went toward Sodom: but Abraham stood yet before the LORD. And Abraham drew near, and said...*

- Prevailing against all odds: holding on firm to your destiny requires a measure of the spirit of boldness. Here Jacob was saddled with how he would survive in his journey, and how the blessings he had so laboured for would become manifest in his life. He had lost joy of togetherness and oneness in his home - Genesis 32:24-29: *And Jacob was left alone; and there wrestled a man with him until the breaking of the day. And when he saw that he prevailed not against him, he touched the hollow of his thigh; and the hollow of Jacob's thigh was out of joint, as he*

CHAPTER FOURTEEN

wrestled with him. And he said, Let me go, for the day breaketh. And he said, I will not let thee go, except thou bless me. And he said unto him, What is thy name? And he said, Jacob. And he said, Thy name shall be called no more Jacob, but Israel: for as a prince hast thou power with God and with men, and hast prevailed.

The spirit of boldness is the opposite of the spirit of fear. God had to test Gideon's army, and those who were not bold were the first to be sent out of the race. Are you failing wherever you find yourself? Have people named you 'failure?' Then this message is for you. Be bold and strong and you will see a new strength to achieve glowing inside of you today.

- Boldness brings comfort. Boldness in a leader is what brings comfort to those he oversees and also gives the leader the confidence to communicate his vision clearly. It brings out the truth in a matter - Hebrews 13:6: *So that we may boldly say, The Lord is my helper, and I will not fear what man shall do unto me.* Anybody who is afraid to speak the truth is not bold, and it is only truth that can set us free. When you lie, then you lack the spirit of boldness. Truth is bitter, they say, but when you are empowered with the spirit of boldness then truth becomes manifest in

CHAPTER FOURTEEN

whatever you do. Pray for the spirit of boldness and He will come to your help, to tutor and bring you to the light. Daniel spoke the truth to Nebuchadnezzar and he was delivered from the lion's den. Saint Paul says (2 Corinthians 7:4): *Great is my boldness of speech toward you, great is my glorying of you: I am filled with comfort, I am exceeding joyful in all our tribulation.*

- You dumbfound your accusers. Christ dumbfounded His accusers in the manner He spoke with authority - John 7:26: *But, lo, he speaketh boldly, and they say nothing unto him. Do the rulers know indeed that this is the very Christ?*

- A demonstration of faith. Without faith no one can please God. And we know that Jesus Christ is the same as God the son who Jacob wrestled with; who is an equal of God the father in action - Ephesians 3:12: *In whom we have boldness and access with confidence by the faith of him.* Hebrews 10:19: *Having therefore, brethren, boldness to enter into the holiest by the blood of Jesus.*

- Boldness is a demonstration of righteousness. We all know that our dear Lord and Saviour, Jesus Christ of Nazareth, referred to as the Lion of the tribe of Judah. Lions are bold animals. When you are

CHAPTER FOURTEEN

righteous, you are as bold as a lion and you can achieve without measure - no boundaries can hold you down, because you have a brand new fire of righteousness burning in you. Intimidation is a product of fear, and fear is bred by the acts of sin we have indulged in. Many of us find it difficult to correct evil because we are guilty of sin already. When we are afraid to speak or communicate our ideas, check very well, we may be under the influence of unrighteous deed before God. If we also run away and are afraid of someone running us down or dominating us, then we should be careful, evil may be in our hands, for the Bible says (Proverbs 28:1): *The wicked flee when no man pursueth: but the righteous are bold as a lion*. But we can plead with the Lord because He is our source of boldness - Ephesians 3:12 *In whom we have boldness and access with confidence by the faith of him*. And when we do this, we should come with the mindset of repentance - Hebrews 4:16: *Let us therefore come boldly unto the throne of grace, that we may obtain mercy, and find grace to help in time of need*.

- The gift of prophesy: boldness is an attribute of prophets of God. They speak what they hear and see

CHAPTER FOURTEEN

- Isaiah 58:1 *Cry aloud, spare not, lift up thy voice like a trumpet, and shew my people their transgression, and the house of Jacob their sins.* Also in Micah 3:8: *But truly I am full of power by the spirit of the Lord, and of judgment, and of might, to declare unto Jacob his transgression, and to Israel his sin.*

- Needed for evangelism: No evangelist is a frail person. They are all bold because the spirit that lives in them is as bold as a lion - Acts 4:29: *And now, Lord, behold their threatenings: and grant unto thy servants, that with all boldness they may speak thy word.* Ephesians 6:19-20 also confirms this fact: *And for me, that utterance may be given unto me, that I may open my mouth boldly, to make known the mystery of the gospel, For which I am an ambassador in bonds: that therein I may speak boldly, as I ought to speak.*

- Shows preparedness for His second coming: our boldness is an element of our submission to the will of God and how far we are ready to stand till the end - 1 John 4:17: *Herein is our love made perfect, that we may have boldness in the day of judgment: because as he is, so are we in this world.*

CHAPTER FOURTEEN

- Strengthens your ability to pray: Boldness strengthens us when we are weak and getting discouraged about life - Psalms 138:3 *When I called, you answered me; you made me bold ...*

CHAPTER FIFTEEN

GETTING HOLD OF TIME BEFORE THE SUN SETS

Time and tide, they say, waits for no one. It is better to start now than to procrastinate. What will you be remembered for when you depart this Earth – for evil or for good?

When the Lord started me on this journey, little did I understand what destiny had in store for me. To keep me on track, the Lord opened my understanding with the words in Isaiah 42:6,9,16 & 20. On this fateful day, we had finished the evening devotion, in the month of January 2005, when I heard – 'read Isaiah 42.' I asked my wife if she was the one that spoke to me, and she replied

CHAPTER FIFTEEN

– 'No!' still naïve about the ways of the Lord, I picked up the Bible to read. Somehow I was led to read it with my wife who was sitting on a sofa in the sitting room. As I read verse 6: *I the Lord have called thee in righteousness, and will hold thine hand, and will keep thee, and give thee for a covenant of the people, for a light of the Gentiles* – I heard a voice say to me, 'I have called you.' Still reading further, now my hands were already trembling, I came to verse 9: *Behold, the former things are come to pass, and new things do I declare: before they spring forth I tell you of them* – I also heard, ' you are a Prophet to nations.' I was getting drenched in the spiritual waterfall that had been created by the immortal powers that were there, which I couldn't see except the voice that showed that they were present in my sitting room. When I got to verse 16 - *And I will bring the blind by a way that they knew not; I will lead them in paths that they have not known: I will make darkness light before them, and crooked things straight. These things will I do unto them, and not forsake them* – tears of joy ran through my heart; I couldn't control my emotions any more. I was yet surprised why the Lord would choose me to do His work. The promises in verse 16 gave me strength, knowing that

CHAPTER FIFTEEN

He would be with me to carry out my work in His vineyard.

I went further until I got to verse 22: *But this is a people robbed and spoiled; they are all of them snared in holes, and they are hid in prison houses: they are for a prey, and none delivereth; for a spoil, and none saith, Restore* – Then I heard, 'this is your task.'

Was that my destiny before me? Yes it was. Like many people, I had been wondering what my purpose on Earth was until I came to this point of my life. I had contemplated death while growing up. I had felt this life was cruel and unfriendly. I had hated many people because I felt they were just living their lives at the expense of others. And, here was God leading me into His Kingdom of Light, through a path that I had not known.

When in October 2008, 3 years and 9 months after the above encounter, the Lord spoke to me while I was driving and told me that it was time for His work to commence, I was taken aback. Why? I was yet to understand what God's call was all about. I tried to seek counselling from people, but the more I did this the more confused I was getting. Then I made up my mind to book an appointment with a pastor – and I heard, 'don't go

CHAPTER FIFTEEN

anywhere you will be polluted, I will train you for six years.' I saw the form of the one that spoke to me beside and behind my shoulder – he was a man and he told me he was also going northward to set up another church. I was afraid to turn, but then I sensed that he had left after speaking to me. I was afraid still, but I managed to proceed to my office.

Some days later as I was driving, somebody wanted me to give them a lift to where I was going, and as I tried to clear off the road to park, I heard a voice from the right-hand side of the back passenger seat of my sedan: 'Move on, I want us to be alone – I want to have a word with you.' Several discussions ensued between us, and I was getting deeper in the spirit, and the boldness to carry on with this work went on and on. One night in the same period, around November 2008 or so, I was in a dream and I saw a multitude of policemen, soldiers and house helps and cooks in my house, and all busy doing one thing or the other. There was tight security, and I was wondering what it was for. It was then it dawned on me that my home had become the abode of the hosts of heaven who had been dispatched to help me carry out the work of the Lord. Then in another vision, I lay on my bed, and I was carried into a worship environment. It

CHAPTER FIFTEEN

seemed as though the people were waiting for me. It was a wonderful place and a sight to behold. Then, I heard a voice – 'you are abandoning my work.' I was getting more confused. There are several other visions and revelations which I cannot put in this book, as they are to be written when the time comes.

The training finally started. The first training was to get me on track into the journey I was about to embark on, and the picture before me was of a man in a boat, alone with a paddle in his hand, sailing through rough waters and heading to a place in the distance. The clouds covered him and it was as if there was no demarcation between the heavens and the waters he was sailing on. The subject of that training was contained in a book – *Existing in the Supernatural*. And I learnt, I could now preach the word and teach it a little. The wisdom was coming and rushing in with much enthusiasm. I had students who were even more eager to learn from someone who had just been called by God. The Lord helped me with lots of information through the stories I would hear from people. The encouragement was also coming from those that would listen to me and they would say that I was teaching like some great servant of God.

CHAPTER FIFTEEN

While I was still getting soaked in the euphoria of being a published author, I heard a voice on the 19th of December 2009 say, 'The Altar in Golgotha.' What sort of statement was this? I asked to know. I was led into an exploration that changed my life – I had a perfect understanding of the works of Salvation and how the Lord had helped me with His precious blood, saving me from all the antics of the devil. Then we were building the church and when it was time to raise an Altar there, I knew exactly what to do. And the night the Altar was raised, the building was filled with His Shekinah, and fear entered into the hearts of all that were there. The truth had come to stay, and I understood that the path of the Lord is a path of continuous spiritual awe.

Later I would write *How Good and Large Is Your Land?* and *Born to Blossom*. These two books followed one after the other in quick succession. The contents were too practical for me to comprehend. I was wondering how I could achieve all that was posited in these two books, with unquestionable facts from the Bible, knowing that if I did, I had come to the pinnacle of life achievement and success. This thought was enveloping me daily.

Then I was started on another knowledge tour. This gave birth to the book *Battles Beyond the Physical*. This

CHAPTER FIFTEEN

book put to remembrance some of the evil practices I had heard and seen while growing up. It opened up a lot of spiritual warfare secrets, and how to overcome them. There were 'Dos and Don'ts' to adhere to if I did not want to be entangled in the spiritual net of the devil. The book explored several spiritual issues that affect many of us on Earth – from the influence our ancestral gods and goddesses to the associations we have with people, and how these have affected our destinies. It was an exhaustive discussion on spiritual warfare. Now I was getting enlightened on the spiritual journey I had undertaken to unravel the mysteries of life, a call of a lifetime. The testimonies were now seen around. My parents had converted from idolatry to Christianity. I was also getting more favour now wherever I went.

I became suddenly sick, and all medications I was given seemed ineffective. This was in 2011. Then one morning, I heard a voice say, 'Feel free to be free.' I was going to the car park to drive my car to the church, while this voice kept repeating itself in my head. I wondered what it was, but it finally became a training opportunity by my teacher – the book *The Path To Absolute Freedom* was born. It is this book that set me on the ladder I am standing on today – the hope of salvation. The centre

CHAPTER FIFTEEN

message was that the moment you are set free by Jesus, you are free forever. Having a headache or body pain is not the issue. These will go. Having the challenges of unemployment and hunger is not the issue – they are a test of faith. My boldness became firm. I was indeed, standing on the rock – my firm foundation. While I rejoiced at this discovery of life, I heard another voice – 'The man God made.'

I prepared a message on this topic in 2011 also, but later, after getting to know that it was another journey into the world of knowledge, understanding and wisdom from the Lord, I yielded to the opportunity. The book *The Man God Made* started me on another level of wisdom quest. Was I becoming mature? Yes of course! My confidence in addressing issues was becoming strong. The pulse in me was beating with the rhythm of the spiritual. I was gradually becoming a servant of God that the world would soon celebrate, as one with wisdom from the most high God.

This book gave me lots of assignments to carry out, behaviourally and spiritually, and I knew that if I obeyed all that the book preached, I wouldn't find it difficult to achieve my destiny before the Lord. This was also when, after knowing that I could talk to a larger audience with

CHAPTER FIFTEEN

confidence, I decided to publish the book for an international audience.

Though my wisdom had increased, I was still having challenges in my marriage. This started me on another learning experience. After hearing a voice in 2009, I had started to write a marriage book that would address marital issues. God taught me and I learnt what marriage was all about, and how I could make my marriage work. The centre point in the book was that marriage was a calling unto God, and a ministry to fulfil before the Lord, and if this is the case, it has to be treated as sacred and given the utmost respect and regard as the institution deserves. Marriage is not fun as many have seen it to be, rather is it a contract. It is rather a means through which the Lord is taking ownership of this Earth from the hand of evil.

To put this wisdom to test, I started applying what the book preaches. My wife also kept a copy under her pillow – and the book worked. The Lord showed His awesome power in restructuring marriages. My home was getting better. I have learnt patience, and my wife was now won to my side. She became very supportive and willing to be there for me, while I had also learnt to stop pushing my heavy weight against all her wishes, as the

CHAPTER FIFTEEN

man in the house. We put the wisdom of the Lord to work and we are still learning. And in March 2014, we started *Singles Seeking Marriage Fellowship (SSMF)*, where we both now teach young people what marriage is all about, using the book as our guide. And the result is splendid.

My home was at peace, but I was having challenges with the administration of the church. In 2012 I had a kind of rebellion among those I thought were supporting me. They had wanted to push their weight of ignorance against the call of God. They had rebelled against everything the Lord was doing. They wanted fun. They wanted money. They wanted miracles. They wanted all the things the devil would offer – freedom to misbehave in the house of God. Then I heard a voice as I battled with all these in my heart – 'leave the church administration, only come to preach on Sundays – get so-and-so to handle this and that, also tell your wife to withdraw.' I obeyed, and then I was led to write a book on leadership. This was when the book *Leadership – An Eagle-Eye Perspective* was born. It has been a book that offers solutions to leadership issues. The moment I learned this leadership secret, I organised a leadership class for those working with me in the church. The information contained wasn't palatable to them and they

CHAPTER FIFTEEN

were no longer having their way, because the Bible evidence was staring them in the face. One after another, they left the class, and I heard a voice – 'stop the class now'.

Closely following this was training I had on some deep spiritual truths which showed that though we may be gifted, we need the anointing of the Lord to ensure that these gifts shine. This is the opinion discussed in the book *Gifted and Anointed*. With this book now in my hand, and the lessons I had learnt from it, I was stronger and ready to face anyone who confronted me demanding evidence for why I was doing what I do. With this understanding that all gifts and talents are beautified by the anointing, and knowing that I already had the anointing, I decided to record a musical album. This led to my first musical album – *Breaking Through*. It has been a success. I have also recorded two other albums soon to hit the airwaves – *Smile Again* and *The Release*, with the message of salvation.

I also wrote a book called *Subject of Love – A Discourse*, with a bid to understand what love truly is, so that I would learn to live by its doctrine and have a life filled with the echoes of love. This has also been widely appreciated, and it is a book that has also been of tremendous help to

CHAPTER FIFTEEN

me as I walk this path with the Lord. The church is now at peace, and my home is also at peace.

The Lord now took me through another learning experience, and this time on the mystery of His kingdom here on Earth, so that I would know how to work in a structured pattern. This is the essence of which my twelfth book, *The Mystery of the Kingdom of God on Earth*, was written. This book lays down the manner of the kingdom and what God expects to see. It explains who a servant of God is and His authorities and limitations. The book also lays down the duties of the wife of the servants of God and the various departments in the church. What do you think is happening here? The Lord is perfecting His purpose in my life.

And now this book, *Understand Your Destiny*, has come to open up the reason behind all this trainings that has now lasted for six years. Before all these happened, I had bought a new Bible, lifted it up in the sun, and prayed – 'Lord, I need a new word from you to lead me to my destiny.' Everything about me is working. My success is there for all to see. God is indeed faithful to those who seek Him diligently. I was called into public ministry in the month of October 2008, six years ago, and in 2014, six years later in the month of October also, the

CHAPTER FIFTEEN

dates and the days of the years are exactly the same as they were six years ago. Isn't God wonderful?

If I had rejected the training proposal, I wouldn't have grown this far today. Are you expecting a miracle? The best miracle is in the knowledge that lives inside you. Miracles are good, only when it is needed to take away a burden that had rendered one incapacitated to undergo the teachings of the Lord. If our quest for miracles is to heal us and then we would relax without going further to follow the teachings of the Lord, then it won't be long before we become empty and the devil will afflict us with more soul-perishing ailments and conditions of distress.

If we look into verse 16 of Isaiah 42, which I quoted earlier, we would see that the Lord's promise to hold my hand and make darkness light before me is being achieved through the learning I am receiving, which has turned into the books I have written so far. If you want the Lord to teach you, get a notebook, kneel down and pray that He should hold your hand and lead you through the path you have not known, and you are on your way to fulfilling your own destiny.

You must now put together a five-year destiny-moulding plan. The first years would be to know yourself and your environment. Knowing yourself has to do with

CHAPTER FIFTEEN

your ability to sincerely scrutinize the person you see in the mirror when you look into it. You must be able to tell the person the truth of what is required to succeed. This frank discussion is sometimes difficult to have, especially with our individual egos pushing for recognition from the inside. The moment we recognise and respect this egocentric voice, we are on the way to our downfall. Our environment includes our parents, friends, enemies, the news going round in the world, the opportunities to excel in the world and especially within our localities first, the information in the social media etc. Most of the skills I have learnt today were gotten from the internet – I just do a search and I start learning. Many young people waste precious time chatting about immoral topics over the internet.

A young man once looked into his parents' library, and seeing all the books they had read, he asked to know why he should attend school, because as far as he was concerned, they had read all that he should have read, and this was the reason he was always wasting his time on the internet and playing games. This is what many young people do – they say to themselves that if Daddy and Mummy read this much and are still unable to make good money, why should they waste their own time schooling? Such ideas will only lead to laxity and destruction.

So the first year is a time to ask several questions about your life – this is the year when you will also identify what you think you can do better. You find out available opportunities for training, sponsors, etc. Your ability to interpret the world from the news you read, see and hear daily will help you to know which direction the world is going. Here you need the help of a counsellor. You will also need to optimise your relationship with God, and if this is well done, you should be able to have the spiritual counselling of your pastor. Then you will need a mentor who is strong in the area you are trying to get into, so that you may be kept abreast of the times. All this requires diligence, sincerity and humility on your part. Don't forget that successful people are busy people and don't have time to waste. So, before you meet them, get all your facts at your fingertips and let them know that you have done good enough research, with evidence and confidence written all over you.

From the second year forward you should implement, monitor, review and amend. So we would say that the first year is for **scouting**. The second year is for **implementation,** the third year for **monitoring,** the fourth year for **reviewing** our progress, and the fifth year would be for **amending** the plan for greater exploits. We therefore now have our five-year destiny-moulding plan in our palm: **Scout, Implement, Monitor, Review and Amend (SIMRA).** All through these processes, you must **Learn**, **Understand** and **Adapt** (LUA), while you spend time to also **Know** people, **Invest** in them, and **Retain** their support (KIR). These have helped me, and I am convinced that these principles will also be of help to you.

Don't forget that you must 'make hay while the sun shines.' This is what I mean by 'getting hold of time before the sun sets.'

Before we end this discussion, I want to live you with this wisdom, as written in my book *How Good And Large Is Your Land?*: *Move with the ball and drive with your heart. That's the rule of the game. Keep on moving. Dream your success. Work your success. Walk like a lion. Smile like an achiever. This is what it takes to move into your land of abundance.*

Shalom!

COVENANT CONFESSION

If you are not born again, you may have read this book as literary material and will not receive the spirit it carries. You can make a decision to correct that now by saying this covenant confession:

Lord Jesus, I know now that you died for my sins. I believe and confess you as my Lord and Saviour. Please come into my life and dwell inside of me.

If you just said this confession, you should locate a spirit-filled church to fellowship with them – let the pastor know you just gave your life to Christ and you will be directed on what to do next. Salvation is a personal race and you must be serious about it.

You can also call us through the numbers below: +234-8076190064; +234-8086737791. Or send us an email at: christmovementinternational@gmail.com

OTHER BOOKS BY THE SAME AUTHOR

1. Existing In The Supernatural
2. The Altar In Golgotha
3. How Good and Large is your Land?
4. Born To Blossom
5. Battles Beyond The Physical
6. The Path To Absolute Freedom
7. The Man God Made
8. Aspects of Marriage
9. Leadership – An Eagle-Eye Perspective
10. Gifted and Anointed
11. The Subject of Love – A Discourse
12. Mystery of the Kingdom of God on Earth
13. The Nonsense of War

ABOUT THE AUTHOR

Pastor Oghenethoja Umuteme encountered God the day he was baptised at St Stephen's Anglican Church, Owhelogbo Delta State, when he received a warm feeling in his heart as he confessed the Lord Jesus as His lord and personal saviour. His birth was surrounded with mysteries – he was born to a mother who had been barren for eight years.

There was hardly anything he said that did not come to pass as he was growing. In 1994 he had a dream in which he received an orange which contained a Bible with a red cover. Events continued dramatically until he started hearing voices telling him to go for rescue, as many souls were heading for destruction. Then it became clear to him that he was being called to carry out the task of restoring mankind back to Jesus.

In January 2006, he heard a voice telling him to read Isaiah 42. On reading to verse 6, he felt a deep force within him and started trembling and a voice said - 'I have called you'. As he read further he was getting immersed in the spirit of God and when he read verse 22, the voice said, 'this is your task'. Then on the 13th of October 2008, he heard a voice while driving: 'Service starts in your house on Sunday.' Events happened that were beyond his understanding and on Sunday 19th October 2008, the first public worship service came to pass.

Pastor Oghenethoja Umuteme is a prolific writer and oversees a leadership foundation, Umuteme Leadership Foundation, which he uses to teach good leadership and a School of Ministry to empower church leaders. A member of the Nigerian Society of Engineers, he has eleven years' work experience in the oil and gas industry in different pipeline engineering functions – design, procurement, fabrication, construction, integrity management, maintenance and operation. A gospel musician with a recorded album, *Breaking Through*, he is also the Founder and Senior Pastor at Royal Diamonds International Church, Port Harcourt, Nigeria. He is an established teacher of the word of God and a prophet to the nation, as shown by his books. Using his crusade ministry, Giant Strides World Outreach Crusade, Pst.

Oghenethoja reaches people with the undiluted word of salvation. And as a prophet to the nations, he has declared prophecies that have been fulfilled – the latest one being the famine that will visit the earth for ten years starting from the year 2017 and ending in 2027. He is also a man of miracles with testimonies said by those who have benefited from the gift of God in his life. As a motivational preacher, he has encouraged many to become successful in their chosen careers. The books God has used him to write have brought healing and encouraged many all over the world with testimonies. Many, including pastors, have also used these books as teaching and counselling materials. A time with him is a time filled with wisdom, joy and humour. He is often referred to as *'primus inter pares.'* His wife, Mrs. Umuteme Adokiye Obele, who supports him in this call of God upon his life, has borne him children – Elomezino, Aghoghomena and Ewevino.

www.ingramcontent.com/pod-product-compliance
Lightning Source LLC
Chambersburg PA
CBHW061647040426
42446CB00010B/1621